D1514808

013827558 2

THE REAL
JEEVES

THE REAL
JEEVES

**THE CRICKETER WHO GAVE HIS LIFE FOR HIS COUNTRY
AND HIS NAME TO A LEGEND**

BRIAN HALFORD

Pitch Publishing
A2 Yeoman Gate
Yeoman Way
Durrington
BN13 3QZ
www.pitchpublishing.co.uk

A CIP catalogue record is available for this book from the
British Library

ISBN-13: 978-1-90917-862-5

Typesetting and origination by Pitch Publishing.
Printed and bound by CPI Group (UK) Ltd, Croydon, CR0 4YY

Contents

For Mary

Foreword

BY DENNIS AMISS (former Warwickshire and England cricketer)

IT GIVES me great pleasure to be asked to write this foreword for Brian Halford's book on Percy Jeeves. I remember hearing about Percy from 'Tiger' Smith, who was one of my coaches at Edgbaston and, as a former Warwickshire and England player, one of the true all-time Bears greats. Tiger always said what a fantastic all-rounder Percy was and that, if he hadn't been killed in the Great War in 1916, he could have gone on to play for England and been one of Warwickshire's, and possibly England's, greatest ever players.

Percy, said Tiger, was a real gentleman and very modest despite his huge talent but died, like so many others, in the Battle of the Somme, giving his life for his country. What a loss, not only to his family but to the game of cricket and to Warwickshire.

Percy Jeeves was born in Yorkshire and, after spending two years qualifying for the Bears, played for Warwickshire in the championship in 1913 and 1914. He was a brilliant all-rounder and so many people enjoyed watching him play during those seasons. He shone for Warwickshire, then when he was called up to play for the Players against the Gentlemen, he bowled out a star-studded Gents batting line-up at The Oval to win the match for his team.

The sky seemed the limit for Percy and he might well have played for England in 1914 if there had been any Test matches that summer. Instead, war was declared before he had a chance. In his 50th and last first-class match for the Bears, Percy bowled out Surrey (including Tom Hayward and Jack Hobbs) to bring victory over the champions at Edgbaston. But the war was already underway.

In this book, Brian delves into the full detail of Percy's excellence as a cricketer, as a boy in Goole and then as a young man in Hawes and at Warwickshire. Then comes the advent of war and the tragic path that took Percy to his untimely death at the age of only 28 on Saturday 22 July 1916.

Percy played 50 first-class matches, scoring 1,204 runs, mostly in bold, attacking style, and taking 199 wickets at 20.03 each. Tiger told me that he kept wicket in all of those matches. How I wish now I had listened to Tiger more about Percy Jeeves – one of cricket's truly gifted players.

Percy's memory will live on forever as one of Warwickshire's finest players, albeit in such a short career. Who knows, he might have played alongside that other great Bears all-rounder Frank Foster for England but for the war.

It was left to P.G. Wodehouse to make famous the name Jeeves after he saw him play in a county match at Cheltenham in 1913. Wodehouse was so impressed both by Percy's attire and the way he played the game that he used his name for his famous character who possessed exactly the attributes of the real Percy Jeeves.

I am delighted that the story of the wonderful cricketer who was the inspiration for that character has now been fully told in Brian's splendid book. Now the real Jeeves, who should have played for his country but instead died for his country, has the recognition he richly deserves.

Foreword
BY MILES JUPP (actor, comedian and writer)

I FIRST met Brian Halford at Lord's in 2006. I had gone to meet a journalist friend and Brian was another of the handful of them ricocheting around the vast media centre attempting to report on that season's County Championship Division One encounter between Warwickshire and Middlesex.

It was a chilly and attritional day but there were runs for Ed Smith and Owais Shah. Brian's chief concern, as I recall, was finding somewhere to sleep for the night. A few of us ended up at the Lord's Tavern and then later the Maida Vale Marriott where the Warwickshire lot were staying. I remember looking up and seeing the likes of Jim Troughton, Nick Knight and Mark Greatbatch.

Someone, somehow, sorted Brian out with a bed. I headed off eventually up the Kilburn High Road a little unsteady on my feet but reflecting that this was how I hoped the county cricket scene might be – a relaxed, genial atmosphere off the pitch, and the local reporter mixing freely with the players.

I first came across the name Jeeves at the start of the 1990s when the excellent ITV adaptation began. I had been, until then, quite oblivious to the work of Wodehouse. But watching a couple of episodes soon led me to reading the books themselves and I was immediately enraptured by the witty, mischievous, smart and silly tales. All of Wodehouse's work has brought me great joy (and as a lover of cricket, one might say that Psmith should be a more natural fit) but it is the Bertie Wooster stories that have remained quite my favourite. And at the heart of them all is, of course, the smooth, urbane and – despite the impervious features – cunning Jeeves.

I did not know, until Brian wrote to me, who this literary Jeeves was named after. What an extraordinarily striking and impressive fellow Percy Jeeves must have been to so capture the imagination of the great P.G. Wodehouse.

One can make a number of assumptions about the qualities Jeeves the cricketer must have had, based on appellation alone. I picture him as having great stillness and poise at the crease and know that he would surely be quite immune to the slings of what our Australian friends term "psychological disintegration".

Somehow, though, he would always be one step ahead of the bowler at all times. He would use the pace of the ball well, but always be able, when called upon, to execute decisive, hard blows. His leg glances and cut shots could only ever be described as "deft".

I see him as being something of a rhythm bowler, possessing great economy of movement, and I rather fancy the thought of him announcing his approach to the bowling crease with a gentle cough. As a fielder he would offer quiet, helpful suggestions to his captain as they passed each other between overs: "It occurs to me, Sir, that this fellow has hands which are rather on the hard side. Might a catcher positioned at silly mid-off be worthy of consideration?"

These qualities, though, are just the works of my imagination. What Brian deals with are facts. Percy Jeeves was not just a cricketer and the inspiration for a great literary character. As this book will tell you, he was so very much more than that; and a man whose life story, short but rich, deserves to be told and also to be read.

Foreword

BY KEITH MELLARD (great nephew of Percy Jeeves)

IN 2000, Audrey and I had been married for 40 years. As we couldn't be sure of getting to 50 years we decided to celebrate by staying in the same hotel we had honeymooned at in Paris, 40 years before. When we looked into it, it was too expensive and we abandoned the idea. However, we hadn't bargained for our children. They clubbed together, booked us into the hotel and reserved first-class seats on the Eurostar.

We have friends in Amiens. We knew that Percy Jeeves was commemorated on the memorial at Thiepval, along with an astonishing number of other men who were named as lost in the Battle of the Somme. The saddest thing was that many of these soldiers were not buried in graves, as identification of remains has been impossible, so they were named on the monument only.

Some graves left us wondering about who had been found. They are marked: "Known unto God".

Enquiries were made with our friends as to how we could visit Thiepval. Their reply was for us to go to the Gare du Nord in Paris, buy tickets for Amiens and they would meet us at the station, which they did. We hadn't realised how close to Amiens the monument at Thiepval was.

We went to the monument with our friends and their eldest son, Guillaume. As there are something like 70,000 names on the monument we expected some difficulty in finding Percy's name. It was the first name I recognised as we approached the front of the monument. Guillaume, who had previously visited the site with his school, showed us the book with Percy's name in it, kept in a bronze cupboard built into the structure.

Why did we want to go? My family were proud of Percy. I grew up with stories about him from his brother, my grandfather, Alick Jeeves. I felt as if I knew him. We were proud of his sporting achievements, and noted his connection with 'Plum' Wodehouse only in passing. As a boy I remember thinking that my family's claims that the Jeeves in the *Jeeves and Wooster* books was named after Percy was just them trying to find some sort of distinction that we weren't entitled to! Heaven help me, that view was corrected when I heard P.G. Wodehouse being interviewed on his 90th birthday on the radio.

Alick, in his quiet way, was a remarkable man. He took me to cricket matches at all the grounds where Yorkshire played, and I saw most of the great cricketers of that era (1940s and 1950s), including the great tourists of that time. Even as an old man, he could spin the ball so fiercely that it looked oval as you tried to play it. He had been good in his day too. Percy was better though. Alick always thought it was hilarious that a man who went on to bowl out the great Jack Hobbs (twice) and Herbert Sutcliffe, as well as many other great batsmen, was rejected by Yorkshire.

As far as I know, I am the first and only member of the family to visit Thiepval. The experience moves me to this day. Not just with regard to Percy, a man I never met, but all the others ground up in the Somme mincer. Those, I didn't know, but feel for. All that unknown potential destroyed in days.

I have always been very proud of Percy and his great talent which was to remain so sadly unfulfilled and I am delighted that Brian has written this book to bring to light his tragic story and those of many thousands like him.

Acknowledgements

RESEARCHING THE story of a chap who led a short and largely unchronicled life, mostly more than 100 years ago, is a tricky project in which all assistance is hugely appreciated so I offer the warmest thanks to numerous people who helped in various ways.

Firstly, to Keith Mellard, grandson of Percy Jeeves's brother Alick. I am sure Keith was pretty taken aback to receive a call out of the blue from some bloke inquiring about his great uncle, but it was soon clear that he is rightly proud of Percy. Keith offered invaluable assistance and I was delighted that a member of Percy's family was involved. All that I have learned about Percy Jeeves during research for this book indicates that he was a man whom anybody would be proud to call a relative.

Keith (a gifted sculptor) was also kind enough to write a foreword for this book so many thanks to him for that.

Forewords are also supplied by Dennis Amiss and Miles Jupp. Dennis needs no introduction and did not hesitate to contribute some words regarding a man about whom he heard plenty while emerging as a player at Edgbaston in the 1960s. That one of Dennis's mentors, the great Tiger Smith, played with and admired Percy binds together two men who are indisputable all-time greats of Warwickshire cricket and one who may well have become one.

Miles's work as an actor, writer and comedian is known to many and I am grateful that he took time out of his busy schedule to read the manuscript and write a thoughtful piece. As a passionate cricket-lover and P.G. Wodehouse fan, Miles's input is most apt.

Any direct link with Percy Jeeves was invaluable so I was amazed to discover one right on the Edgbaston doorstep when John Bridgman told me his father Charlie was a close friend of Percy. The doyen of Warwickshire's committee, John has a million anecdotes to tell and most end with a punchline and a chuckle but his recollections of his dad's admiration for Percy – especially that his father, throughout a long and happy life, never had another friend as close as the one he lost at High Wood in July 1916 – were truly moving.

Another connection with Percy came through his scrapbook and copies of *Wisden* which are now in the possession of journalist and author David Frith. I extend many thanks to David for allowing me to see the books and also some letters and to reproduce images of them in this book. David acquired them some years ago from Harold Jeeves,

Percy's younger brother, so thanks are also due, posthumously, to Harold for his foresight in ensuring the precious items were delivered to safe keeping.

My gratitude goes too to Goole. During my visits there everyone I met was welcoming and helpful. I appreciate the guidance, in particular, of Margaret Howard, Carole Howard, Harvey Tripp, Susan Butler, Edna Austin and Chris Laidler of Boothferry Family and Local History Group, Pat Penistone at Goole Library, Paul Lewis and Janet Tierney at the museum and Andy Morris and Eric Lawton of Goole Town Football Club.

Sincere thanks also to:

David Baynham at the Royal Regiment of Fusiliers Museum (Royal Warwickshire), to which thanks also for allowing use of excerpts from the battalion diaries.

Matthew Baker, ranger at Sutton Park, and Birmingham Library Service for permission to use images.

Norman Murphy, chairman of the P.G. Wodehouse Society.

Joan Rutledge and Noel Rogers for genealogy expertise.

Kate Balfour, Paul Lazenby and Chris Waters for advice on the manuscript.

Phil Britt, Gervald Frykman, David Hardy, Roger and Lesley Halford, Kevin Halford, Kevin Howells, Phil O'Farrell, Neil Smith, Mark Woodward, Sue Hurrell and Peter Wynne-Thomas.

Information has been taken from the *Birmingham Post & Mail, Goole Times, Dewsbury Times* and *Yorkshire Post* newspapers and the following books: *The Gorway Story* (E.J.A. Cook), *Cricket Calling* (Rowland Ryder), *The History of Warwickshire CCC* (Jack Bannister), *The Railway Workers 1840–1970* (Frank McKenna), *A Who's Who of Warwickshire CCC* (Robert Brooke), *F.R. Foster: The Fields Were Sudden Bare* (Robert Brooke), *Warwickshire CCC – A History* (G.W. Edgell and M.K.F. Fraser), *Wisden Cricketers' Almanack, Birmingham Pals* (Terry Carter) and *The Hell They Called High Wood* (Terry Norman) as well as the minute-books of Warwickshire CCC's general committee.

Checking facts from events more than a century ago is not always easy and there were times when different highly-respected sources disagreed, but I have done my best.

I thank Pitch Publishing who have done their customary professional job and Duncan Olner for an excellent cover design.

And finally, Mary Bonner whom I thank for, well…everything.

Introduction

SHORTLY AFTER starting work for the *Birmingham Post & Mail* in 2000 I became aware of Percy Jeeves. His career as a cricketer for Warwickshire interested me straight away for its success and brevity. I am intrigued by sportsmen who flit briefly into public view, especially at a high level, then vanish.

As I learned more about Percy, two things became clear. He was an all-rounder of the highest quality. And his death, aged 28, in the First World War, was a desperate tragedy. The fact that P.G. Wodehouse named his famous character after this man added to the fascination and when it emerged that Percy Jeeves appeared to be that rarest sort of human being – one about whom nobody has a bad word to say – I thought his story should be told.

That story's compilation has not quite been a 13-year project (it lay dormant at times as the day-job got in the way) but has been a slow-burner during which the more I learned about Percy, the more I admired him for his cricket talent, his humility and the patriotism and courage which cost his life.

Percy's death was no less tragic than many others during the First World War but his story is a microcosm of the sickening waste entailed in that conflict. Many men had as much to give as Percy – but none had more. The lives of many ended in circumstances as appalling and hopeless as Percy's – but none more so.

I have read quite widely about the First World War but had never before seen battalion diaries and it is these small tomes, written with such simplicity and understatement, which bring the soldiers' hideous ordeal into the sharpest focus. At times, life was so unpleasant in terms of hunger, cold and filth that even the omnipresent mortal danger became a secondary concern.

In the pages that follow there is very little from Percy Jeeves himself. During his brief cricket career, it appears that he gave only one interview. It is reproduced in full but, that apart, his feelings can only be imagined as he grows up in Goole, fledges as a cricketer in Hawes, shines at Edgbaston then joins the army, is trained and sent to France with the 15th Battalion, Royal Warwickshire Regiment.

While many people offer opinions about Percy's cricketing prowess, on his military service there is, of course, no commentary. And while Percy's movements in the army can be traced from his first day's training at Sutton Park to the fatal night at High Wood, the battalion diaries list the movements of the men as a unit. Of Percy himself there is no mention. This does place limitations on the biography but I hope without detracting too much from it.

The ordeal of the men fighting in France is clear and, while there is a temptation to speculate on how they felt at various times (I think it is reasonable, for example, to assume that Percy and his comrades were thinking of home on Christmas Day), I have kept speculation to a minimum.

Essentially, this book traces Percy Jeeves's life and experiences as comprehensively as possible but it is the story of him, not from him. I hope I have done him justice.

Brian Halford, Warwick, May 2013

1.

A four-in-hand – Prevention of Singing Act – The Grasshoppers spring into life – Superhuman subtlety

ON 8 June 1907, Goole Cricket Club's first XI were dismayed to find themselves without a game. It was a glorious day, perfect for cricket, the players reflected as they cast about at home or approached the end of their shifts at the docks on Saturday morning. A terrible waste.

Then news filtered through that some chaps from Adlingfleet, a village nine miles out of town, fancied a game. Adlingfleet had no formal cricket team or even a pitch. But, down in the rural depths of Marshland, the villagers had a field to spare, a bit of kit and a lot of enthusiasm so they invited Goole to join them on a beautiful afternoon in East Yorkshire.

Off went the men of Goole, crammed into a four-in-hand with schoolteacher and captain William Appleyard at the reins. Along Bridge Street the vehicle carried its happy cargo, through docks still busy on a Saturday afternoon and across the river bridge before the horses gathered pace along winding Swinefleet Road. After Swinefleet the route opened out into flat farmland, the cricketers holding on tight as the vehicle sped through tiny Reedness. They whizzed past the imposing church of St Mary Magdalene, Whitgift, and on through sunlit pasture land, the road running parallel to the river for miles either side of Ousefleet before slowing for a sharp bend to the right. The lane careered away from the river and took another sharp twist right then another to the left where it became Hoggard Lane. This was Adlingfleet and the horses could get some rest and the men some cricket.

Goole first XI were no great shakes on the field and, as illustrated by this gap in their fixture list, a haphazardly organised lot off it. They did not play in a league and won few matches. But the men loved the game and, at the end of a hard working week, mostly on the docks and railways, they climbed from the carriage bursting to play.

Among them was 19-year-old Percy Jeeves. Third son of Edwin, a passenger guard with the Lancashire and Yorkshire Railway, Percy had not long been taken on by the railway himself as a dock labourer. He was cricket-mad and ready for fun, just like the rest. But in one way he was very different from his team-mates. Whereas their cricket prowess came in at various points between half-decent and hopeless, Jeeves was good. Very good.

Within his slender frame was the stuff of greatness, it was to transpire. But all that concerned Percy and his pals on this impromptu journey into the Marshland countryside was to have a game of cricket.

Waiting for them in Adlingfleet were no talented cricketers but farmers, labourers, blacksmiths – and magnificent hosts. The visitors disembarked to the warmest welcome and, fortunately, among them was one non-player, the *Goole Times* sports correspondent who wrote under the name 'Spectator'. Thanks to him, an account of the trip still exists.

Six days later he described in the paper the Goole team's visit to Adlingfleet; a day of cricket in its purest form. Cricket for cricket's sake. Cricket for the joy of it.

"The Goole first team found themselves without a match, much to the discomfort of members of the second team, who, in such circumstances, are often expected to get off the earth and let the seniors play their match for them. Happily, this was not the case last weekend, for at the eleventh hour a rumour spread that cricket was to be had in limited quantities down Adlingfleet way, where the scientists come from, or go to. Confirmation of this was to be found about two o'clock on Saturday afternoon when a four-in-hand, or was it one-out-of-hand, drove away towards Bridge-street.

"It was a somewhat compact affair, but the dispositions were excellent in their way. The vehicle was in the charge of a classical driver, who umpires for a living and fills in his time worrying small boys into making mistakes in arithmetic. The players who were prospecting for cricket were, however, utterly reckless. They felt that they were merely adding to the ordinary risks of the game, and if the umpire was bent on saying 'out' they knew they must bow to his decision, especially if he emphasised his point by driving across a hedge or two.

"Once out in the country, the passengers threw off disguises – one had concealed himself behind a Woodbine – and it was seen that several of the brightest and most beautiful stars of the Goole firmament were of the party. There followed a debate, the agenda being as follows:

Stopping places.
Prevention of Singing Act.
Sandwiches.
Butter drops.
Name of the team.
Feeding of infants (over 12 stones).
Disposition of passengers' feet.

"With regard to the first item it was decided to stop at Adlingfleet on the motion of a gentleman who stated that in all ranks of life minorities must suffer. The second item resolved itself by close contest with items three and four. The christening ceremony was somewhat drawn out, any mention of the Goole first team being rigorously excluded for fear of ultimate defeat. Eventually it was decided to label, or libel, the team Grass-hoppers although the term 'hoppers' almost led to a recrudescence of the debate on stopping-places. The question of the feeding of infants was promptly dispatched, the vote for ham and eggs being practically unanimous. The last item on the agenda was amicably settled by two of the passengers consenting to hang their extremities outside the waggonette.

"The debate finished in time to allow of the exchange of salutes of a personal character with several Swinefleet agricultural gentlemen who were discovered holding up a wall with complete success. At Whitgift the driver had a short consultation with his untamed steed, which led to the historic old church being hurriedly passed, to the great concern of the only scientist in the party. The other Cities of the Plain were merely skirted, and at 3.15 the journey abruptly terminated owing to a brick-wall suddenly springing up in front of the horse. The driver was hurriedly awakened, and the party disembarked.

"Needless to say the cricket was completely in keeping with the rural character of the surroundings. Any player found in flannels was a marked man, and was sharply interrogated as to the last county team he assisted. A double-headed penny thoughtfully handed to the home captain to throw up resulted in the Grasshoppers having choice of innings, and in view of threatening conduct on the part of his team, it was decided to hop first. Whereupon the 'field' spread itself.

"In the opening stages of the game the Grasshoppers failed to hop to any extent, the two Halkons being difficult to get away. Jeeves and Appleyard, however, held the fort with tremendous success. Jeeves actually hit two 'threes' and Appleyard one. Had either of the batsmen clumped a 'four' no doubt the opposition would have left the field in disgust at such a breach of etiquette. The innings closed with the total at 71.

"Adlingfleet commenced badly, Jeeves displaying an almost American spreadeaglism. After repeated warning, he was taken off for not hitting the bat often enough. Afterwards Fletcher and several of the Halkons played well but when, with superhuman subtlety, the Hoppers' captain put Lee on to bowl the innings abruptly terminated in consequence of the unparalleled velocity of the new bowler's trundling."

The match ended with the delightfully irrelevant scores: Goole Grasshoppers 71 all out, Adlingfleet 40 all out. Young Jeeves enjoyed plenty of success. He was joint top-scorer with 17 and then took the first six wickets before being withdrawn from the attack. Victorious and vanquished alike thoroughly enjoyed the occasion and, after a jar or two at close of play, songs and laughter filled the lanes again as the four-in-hand headed back to town.

2.

Jeeves takes eight – Perils of the light railway – Purvis's manly chest – It is resolved to lynch the secretary

S O ENJOYABLE did the men of Goole find their carefree afternoon in Marshland that any repeat would be much-welcomed. An opportunity soon came. Three weeks later they returned deep into the sticks, this time to Luddington.

Before then, rain restricted them to just one first-team match, away to Swanland Manor, a village out east towards Hull. It was not a long journey but an awkward one involving a train to North Ferriby then a mile-long, kit-laden walk uphill from the station. The arduous approach warmed Percy Jeeves up nicely. He took eight wickets as Swanland were skittled all out for 62. Left 55 minutes to chase the runs, Goole sent Jeeves in first and his brisk 15 set them on the way to a rare victory.

Next, enragingly on a rare sunny Saturday in a damp summer, came another blank day in the pre-arranged fixture list. So the Grasshoppers hopped into motion again: destination Luddington, five miles south-west of Adlingfleet.

This time they spared the horses and travelled by train. Nine years earlier, the Goole & Marshland Light Railway had snaked its way out towards the hamlets of Marshland as local businessmen, mostly connected to Goole Farmers' Club, sought to make money from the transport revolution. Make money they did. In 1898, the 13-and-a-half mile line (the first sod was cut by William Halkon of Adlingfleet) cost £57,186 to build. In 1902 it was sold to the London & North-Eastern Railway for £73,500.

The branch line left the main track at Marshland Junction and headed east to Eastoft, Luddington and Fockerby. Stations opened in those villages on 19 August 1903 and closed on 17 July 1933 with the closure of the line, one of numerous quixotic railway ventures of the time which never had a hope of financial viability and, therefore, no long-term future. The Goole & Marshland Light Railway is the humblest of footnotes in the history of railways but it did a job for the Goole Grasshoppers one hazy day in the summer of 1907.

With the Grasshoppers aboard, the huge engine chugged its way through the sunshine across the 120-feet-long bridge over Swinefleet Drain and on into the marshes. It paused at Eastoft where, on a very different day six years earlier, with the land shrouded in fog and darkness, two locomotives collided head on and a driver and a fireman lost their lives. Then it steamed on to Luddington and the little, red-brick station, perched on a slope above the village. The cricketers of Goole walked down the hill between the tall hedges of Mill Lane and turned right into High Street and there was the sports field.

Flat and exposed, the football pitch had players shivering and cursing in winter, but this day was warm and the breeze friendly and the rough plot had been turned into a cricket arena. Twenty-two yards of grass was marked out as a pitch and waiting there was a home team ready to match the hospitality offered by their neighbours from Adlingfleet.

Luddington knew how to host. The village's annual Feast and Sports Day, with a cricket match against Adlingfleet as its central point, was a highlight of the Marshland calendar. Potato-picking, treacle bun-eating and washing competitions, running, bicycle and obstacle races and a tug-of-war were among the sports which accompanied the feast of a sumptuous spread with a hog roast at its heart. Luddington folk liked to entertain. Now, with another Feast and Sports Day not due for very nearly a year, they lavished their attention on Jeeves and his fellow Grasshoppers.

Thanks to Spectator, another heavenly day in Edwardian England, the first and last Luddington Cricket Festival was preserved in print.

"The Goole first team were to have been amongst the unemployed last Saturday afternoon, according to the fixture card, but a recent visit to Adlingfleet bred such a passion for Marshland village cricket that the fixture was filled in with a match at Luddington. I must say that the Luddington Cricket Festival lasts for one day in the year, but that is *THE* day of the season. Those members and friends of the Goole team who braved the perils of a journey on the light railway, whereon the trains stop to meditate on the lightest provocation, came away with a tremendous idea of the hospitality of the natives of Luddington. It was immense. Everything was free but runs, and those had to be worked for amid toil and tribulation.

"The match was played on the show ground, on a specially prepared wicket. The pitch spoke for itself. Had it not been prepared the night before, it would have appeared in all its native loveliness as the haunt of cattle. I must in fairness state that the local enthusiasts picked out the best ridge of the lot whereon to make a wicket. And it 'played' better than it looked, which is not saying much.

"The Goole skipper being away in Devon, and the vice-captain trying to work up his average with the second team, F. Horsnell was duly laden with the cares of captaincy. He returned thanks in the best possible way by saying 'heads' at the psychological moment. And, behold, it was 'heads' whereupon Goole went in to bat.

"The visitors had only ten players but a capable-looking substitute was picked up on the ground. Of the 'sub' more hereafter. The Goole batting was like the curate's egg, good in parts. It was also rotten in parts and half and half at other times. The best innings came from the bat of J. Latham, who played sound cricket all round the wicket. It is rather astonishing that he does not get more runs. His 19 on Saturday last was worth 50 on any other ground.

"H. Purvis also helped himself to runs in good style. On the curiosity of a wicket the ball played all sorts of tricks, sometimes careering gaily heavenward, at others buzzing along the ground in a sly attempt to crawl under the unsuspecting bat. In our happy childhood these were designated 'sneaks' and deserved the name.

"The 'sub' was something of a mystery. He opened a stone-waller, but lashed out at intervals just to keep point and cover in their proper places, as it were. Eventually he lost his wicket through lack of mobility.

"Luddington went in with close on 100 runs to get if they desired to celebrate the feast in appropriate style. Unfortunately for local enthusiasm they fell just short by about 70. Horsnell worried them out in collusion with Purvis at point. The latter, on one occasion, in a moment of abstraction, 'pouched' the ball from off the end of a stone-waller's bat. His activities so upset another batsman that he attempted to cut the ball through Purvis's manly chest. The chest remained intact, whilst the batsman went thoughtfully back to the tent. I really believe Purvis could catch anything – even measles.

"It was while Purvis and Horsnell were juggling together that the Goole 'sub' showed his mettle. His place, nominally, was at mid-off, but he was off on his own most of the time. Red-tape was not for him. He held a roving commission, counter-signed by himself. He supplied the remainder of the team with 'cues' as to the abilities of the incoming batsman. If he took up a position three yards from the bat we assumed that the batsman was a stone-waller. If he disappeared into the adjoining field it was a pretty sound indication that the batsman was capable of carting the ball extensively. When he condescended to stray to his proper place it was a fair assumption that orthodox cricket might be expected. Unluckily, Horsnell and Jeeves did not give the batsmen time to prove any of the sub's theories.

"The match ended in an easy victory for Goole. Afterwards tea was provided for the teams and great was the rejoicing thereat. The victuals disappeared at an alarming rate, and it was unanimously resolved to lynch the Goole secretary forthwith in the event of his failing to book another match with Luddington next season. The teams departed full of enthusiasm and cold beef."

To Goole's total of 86, Luddington had replied with a mere 26. Jeeves took five wickets with extras top-scoring for the home team with seven. Nobody gave a hoot about the result though as the sun set over the rolling fields and two groups of cricket-lovers bade the warmest farewells as the Grasshoppers headed back to the station.

For the next six days these cricket-lovers would follow their favourite sport via the newspapers. Every Friday they would catch up with all the local scorecards from the previous weekend in the *Goole Times,* while national papers enabled them to monitor the county cricket fixtures on a daily basis.

The humble Grasshoppers followed the fortunes of the greats of the Golden Age: Jack Hobbs, C.B. Fry, 'Plum' Warner, Gilbert Jessop and Yorkshire's own George Hirst and Wilfred Rhodes; members of the England team which held the Ashes and had just faced South Africa at Lord's in the visitors' first Test on foreign soil. Great names up there in the cricket pantheon and as far removed as could be from a rough field at Luddington. But one of the Goole Grasshoppers in the carriages trundling homeward at the end of that perfect summer's day would one day play with and against those men. The boy who bowled out Adlingfleet would hit the stumps of Hobbs. The young shaver taken off to prolong the game at Luddington would dismiss Warner and be hailed by the England captain as a Test player in waiting.

3.

Poor circumstances – A move to Sleepy Hollow – Under William Appleyard's wing – Featherstone slag

PERCY JEEVES was born on 5 March 1888 in Earlsheaton, a small textile town on the south-eastern edge of Dewsbury in the West Riding of Yorkshire. There was no cricket in his family background. Jeeves came from humble stock, far removed from the aristocracy and country-house wealth where the sport was first established. His father Edwin, born in Hertfordshire in 1862, worked as a railwayman after moving north in early adulthood to escape poor circumstances. Edwin was brought up in Ickleford, a village just north of Hitchin, first by unmarried aunt Martha and her sister Betsey, both straw plaiters, and then by his widower father Thomas, a farm labourer.

Edwin briefly served as an apprentice barber but decided to seek pastures new and became one of the thousands of men migrating from the countryside to towns and cities to find work in the burgeoning railway industry. At that time, a job on the railways was much-coveted (and for life if you kept your nose clean) and in Dewsbury, Edwin found the steady employment he needed on the Lancashire and Yorkshire Railway.

He met Nancy Garforth, the daughter of textile workers Jeremiah (a woollen spinner) and Christiana (a weaver). Nancy was just 17 years old when, in 1885, she married Edwin and had their first child, Thomas. Two years later came second son Alick and, the following year, a third – Percy. It was a crowded little house and when the latest addition arrived no one speculated that here could be a great cricketer.

More pertinent questions were "how will we feed him?" and "where will we put him?"

Earlsheaton was a busy town with a population of 5,000, many of whom worked in its three woollen mills, churning out blankets and rugs. The Jeeves boys attended the local mixed board school where they picked up their first bats and balls. Alick was a spin bowler but Percy liked to bowl fast – and hit the bat hard. Small but wiry and strong, he had a good eye and timed the ball sweetly but it was only after 1901, when he was moved out of the cricketing hotbed of West Yorkshire to the backwater of the West (now East) Riding, that his talent began to blossom.

Edwin was transferred to Goole, known locally as "Sleepy Hollow" due to its remote location and gentle pace of life. The family took a home in Parliament Street, a tight, narrow thoroughfare lined on both sides by small, terraced houses populated almost entirely by the families of railway workers. One end of Parliament Street joined Boothferry Road, the busy main road into town. At the other was Marcus Street, across which lay the Victoria Pleasure Grounds.

Opened 13 years earlier following Queen Victoria's diamond jubilee, this 200-yard by 150-yard oblong of open space, just over the railway line from the docks, boasted a bandstand, a grandstand and a sports field. Goole Cricket Club played their home matches there and the Jeeves residence, number 77, was two houses from that end of Parliament Street. From a back window, Percy could peer to his right to see what was going on in the Pleasure Grounds. Often he was round there.

After only a few months, Edwin moved his family the short distance to 72 Manuel Street. Parallel to Parliament Street, Manuel Street was 200 yards further west from the town centre and newly-built as part of the expansion of Goole. The two streets were – and remain today – almost identical, tight dormitory roads with serried, red-brick homes, each front door leading directly to the street.

The back gardens were about the length of a cricket pitch, but too narrow and cluttered with outside toilets and coal sheds to allow the Jeeves boys to fit games of football and cricket in there. There was no need, though. They could play in the "ten-foot" – the alleyway beyond the back gate – and there was always the Pleasure Grounds.

Following their move, the journey for Tom, Alick and Percy from home to the sports field had risen from 20 seconds to a whole minute but it was a short commute they took frequently. Right out of home, left into Marcus Street, past Henry Street, across the busier Dunhill Road, past the entry to Parliament Street and over the road through the big iron gates. And out came bat and ball.

Edwin, at 39, now had the job he would hold for the rest of his working life. He was a passenger guard on the Haxey route, a winding 20-mile branch line through the sparse countryside south of the Humber. Nancy looked after the house and the boys, who settled in among 500 infants and 1,000 senior boys and girls at the vast Alexandra Street Board School in the town centre. Each morning, the Jeeves brothers took the 15-minute walk to school, either cutting through the grid of streets in the estate before joining Boothferry Road close to town or walking up Manuel Street then all the way up the busy main street. The latter route took them past Goole Flour Mills and the sprawl of the workhouse to the railway station and the imposing red-brick school which backed on to the station goods yard.

Sport was taken seriously at Alexandra Street. The boys played football and rugby in the winter and cricket in the summer – and 14-year-old Percy found his first mentor, William Appleyard. A schoolmaster of high vocation and a devout cricket-lover, Appleyard was only 26 years old so possessed a youthful energy which bonded him with the boys. Goole born and bred, the eldest of eight children of a blacksmith, he devoted much of his own time to coaching cricket and played for the town club.

Under Appleyard's tutelage, Jeeves led the school team through a fine season. He took 33 wickets at 2.2 runs each, remarkable figures even taking the poor pitches into consideration. With those pitches in mind, barely less impressive was his batting average of 18.50.

Jeeves's all-round influence was clear against arch-rivals Boothferry Road Board School. He took two wickets as the opposition were bowled out for 14 then struck 53 of Alexandra Street's 86.

The school's annual report reflected: "Out of 12 matches played, ten have been won and two lost. The wickets, for the most part, have been very rough and the greatest difficulty has been obtained in obtaining fields at all the schools. In batting, Percy Jeeves has been marvellously consistent, twice having succeeded in passing the half-century and getting into double figures nine times. For 12 innings he scored 223 runs, an average of 18.5. He bowled 55.1-19-73-33, an average of 2.2."

Those bowling figures were eye-catching but, so poor were those pitches, they still put him only third in the list behind H. Pidd (22.2-12-26-16, average 1.6) and H. Thorpe (69.4-22-88-41, average 2.1).

Alongside school cricket, Percy also joined his schoolmaster at the town club and attended regular practices at the Pleasure Grounds. Goole Town Cricket and Lawn Tennis Club ran first and second cricket teams and, while neither played in a league, there was enough enthusiasm to justify the holding of practices every weekday evening. A member's ticket cost five shillings, including admission to all matches, while a playing member's card was seven shillings and sixpence and allowed admission to all matches and practice sessions.

Jeeves practised hard and learned quickly, although there were times when the Pleasure Grounds were, as a venue, less than serene. Steam trains passed no more than 30 yards from one boundary while immediately the other side of the railway was the port with its jungle of water towers, coal hoists, cranes and chimneys servicing vessels which made quite a racket. They also transported all manner of pungent cargo. As Spectator pointed out in one match report, the players had to contend with some appalling stenches:

> "The weather was fair to middling and there were hopes of a good day's cricket but alas cricket was quite spoiled by the trade of Goole. The wind brought along with it engaging perfumes from the funnels of shipping in the docks. Judging from the spicy breezes which blew over Carter Street, some of the steamers must have run short of coal and been reduced to burning the old boots of the crew, together with a stray waistcoat or two thrown in. The Goole ground was a pleasant place to be out of. After a rousing gallop after the bounding leather, one surely deserved more than a lungful of best Featherstone slag."

It is safe to say there were not too many volunteers to field on the dock-side boundary – at pong-on and pong-leg.

4.

"He sent down pure piffle" – The young express bowler – Right-back for Swinefleet – Train trouble

PERCY JEEVES quickly became a regular in Goole's second XI and it was clearly only a matter of time before the boy was mixing it with the men in the first team. His elevation arrived soon after he celebrated his 17th birthday, early in the 1905 season.

The second XI's opening game, at home to Saltmarshe, was rained off but the next, against Hull Church Institute, was played and Jeeves wasted no time getting among the wickets. He took six, including an opening burst in which he "rattled four men out in two or three overs".

A week later he bagged 6-23 to skittle Knottingley for 48. Jeeves's abundant promise was faithfully chronicled by Spectator, though the scribe was not an easy man to impress. When the youngster turned out for Goole Thursday against the Tennis Section and took four wickets, all clean bowled, the reporter was scathing. "Jeeves netted four for 12 but didn't deserve a single wicket," he observed. "He sent down pure piffle. His victims got themselves out."

Two days later, at Snaith, Jeeves's all-round exploits left no scope for complaint. After Goole made 61, of which Jeeves's share was 29, the home side were all out for 38: Jeeves 11.4-5-12-7.

His biggest critic still found room for some advice, however. "Jeeves was top scorer for the visitors," *Spectator* commented. "I hope he will now settle down to play sound cricket instead of hitting out at everything that comes down. It isn't always the man who can hit hardest that makes the biggest score."

The little matter of 7-12 did not evoke comment from the journalist.

Goole's selectors quickly decided that Percy was ready for the first team. The following week, he was elevated to the seniors for the home match with Balby and took the step up comfortably. After going in at number 11 and making 0 not out in a total of 154, Jeeves took three wickets as Balby clung on for a draw at 100/7.

Jeeves's debut also introduced him to the sometimes fractious nature of cricket at first-team level. During the visitors' reply, Spectator noted: "The Balby men were very dissatisfied with one or two decisions of the home umpire and showed their feelings in an unsportsmanlike manner.

"It was quite reminiscent of football at Doncaster," added the scribe, though it is unclear whether his distaste referred more to football, at which there was frequent violence among the spectators in those days, or the town of Doncaster.

Jeeves's second first-team appearance followed against Hull Congos at the Victoria Pleasure Grounds and this time the newcomer unfurled his talents with both bat and ball. A benefit match for Goole's groundsman, Shires, the event was recorded by Spectator with an assiduousness which suggested that he rather enjoyed the sound of his nib scratching. It appears that such abundant detail was vindicated, however, by the level of interest among his readers in cricket as scorecards and reports were submitted each week by dozens of clubs in and around the town.

In 1905, of course, unless a person attended a match, or bumped into someone who had, the only way to find out how the team had fared at the weekend was by getting a paper the following Friday.

In Spectator, the readers of the *Goole Times* had a most diligent and colourful correspondent:

"Shires could not have had a more beautiful day than Saturday last for his benefit and the players could not have had a better pitch to play on. I think he must have slept on the field last week. There was quite a large number of spectators, a hundred tickets being taken at the gate, besides much coin of the realm, and those who sat perspiring round the field saw and highly appreciated a most exciting game – the best played on the Pleasure Grounds for many a long day. The luck of the game fluctuated; first the visitors held the winning hand, then the home men did, and finally when things looked somewhat black for Goole, Duckels and Coverley pulled the game out of the fire and the homesters had the pleasure of winning a great struggle by three runs – their first victory of the season.

"Congos had the luck to win the toss. Hepton and Gibson commenced operations. Horsnell sent down the first over, off which two runs were scored. Jeeves, with the last ball of his over, sent Hepton to the rightabout. Then came a great stand, King and Gibson taking the score to sixty-two before the former was beaten by a beauty from Jeeves. Millard joined Gibson who was playing with great confidence, but put his legs in front of the first ball he received, and had to go.

"Gibson was the only man who seemed to be able to time the young express bowler. Horsnell they scored off pretty easily, knocking thirty-six off him for no wickets. Duckels was tried but, though he bowled well, he had no luck. Finally, the skipper thought he would try Talbot and his thought, being put into execution, proved a lucky one, for this redoubtable trundler took three wickets for nineteen runs. Jeeves came out with a fine analysis – twelve overs, two maidens, thirty-three runs, seven wickets.

"The Congos' score was not by any means a large one on such a grand wicket, but the bowling of the Goole men was good and the fielding even better. Rarely have they given such an exhibition. To see Coverley and Bond sprinting across the field was a rare, welcome sight, and Duckels, in the country, was a marvel – in fact he had a bigger share in winning the match than appears on paper.

"The usual pair opened the Goole innings, but Cooper quickly retired, bowled by one of Fenton's expresses. I should say this bowler is the fastest seen on the Goole ground since the time when J.T. Brown, of Darfield, played here. Horsnell did not improve his average very much. Coverley was very steady, too steady in fact. Had he sprinted across the track as he did in fielding, and had he made all the short runs possible, the home total and his score would have been larger by a round dozen or more. But I must not detract from his performance for, going in second wicket down, he was last out with 34 to his credit. Talbot didn't assist him a bit and, with four down for 34, things didn't look very promising.

"Then Jeeves, not a bit tired from his exertions in bowling, came in and hit to such good effect that the score was increased by 53 before he was dismissed. He had played a plucky innings. Barron made nine, his highest score so far, and then trouble came he, Everett and Naylor being bowled by Cross in four balls. It looked odds on Congos with eight down for 98. Then Smith was unfortunate to play a ball on to his pads, and from them to his wickets, the score then being nine for 102 – 16 to tie and 17 to win.

"Duckels came in the last man – why, goodness knows – and some croakers reckoned the game as good as lost. But he stuck to it manfully and hit two fours while Coverley added seven. It was a two to leg – a pretty hit – by Coverley which decided the game. There was a cheer such as one seldom hears at a cricket match on the Goole field, which told how delighted and how excited the spectators were. The end soon came after this, with Coverley being caught at the wicket in the last over of the match. Duckels carried out his bat for nine. He went in at a critical time, and I heartily congratulate him on his grit."

Goole won by one wicket, overtaking the target of 118 with nine men out before batting on to reach 121 all out. Jeeves took 7-33 and scored 33 crucial runs to unveil himself well and truly as a first-team player.

He received an immediate reminder that cricket is a great character-builder. A week later at Knottingley, Jeeves was wicketless as the home side piled up 230/2. He "batted nicely" for ten, though, as Goole replied with 132/6, and he had quickly became one of the first names written on the first XI teamsheet. He ended the summer of 1905 a first-team regular.

During the following winter, Jeeves was also a regular at right-back for Swinefleet Football Club, a village team three miles east of Goole. Quick and strong in the tackle, he was a tidy footballer and thoroughly enjoyed playing but lacked the natural aptitude at the winter sport which he possessed for cricket. His football helped his cricket, though, by keeping him fit and strengthening him up. While still slightly built, he was gaining power to fuel his natural bowling rhythm and the summer of 1906 saw him excel in a struggling Goole team.

The early weeks of the season were wet. When Hull Wilberforce, named after Hull-born former MP and anti-slavery campaigner William Wilberforce, visited the Pleasure Grounds, it rained heavily and the teams played billiards (at which Jeeves also excelled) instead of cricket. The weather relented for a trip to Beverley but Jeeves's season began poorly with a duck and no wickets as Goole were skittled for 58 before the home side replied with 101/2.

All the rain left the early-season pitches harder than ever to bat upon, though Goole usually found them more treacherous than the opposition. In the return match against Hull Wilberforce at the elegant Jalland's Estate ground, Goole made 64 before the home side compiled

100/7 (Jeeves scored eight and took two wickets). "A visit to Jalland's Estate with its delicately tinted hedgerows and trees, spring flowers and joyous birds, is always a pleasure," reported Spectator, "but the men from Sleepy Hollow provided a most tame and uninteresting exhibition."

Goole were a mediocre side but Jeeves continued to shine. He took 3-18 against Selby, 3-16 against Hull Stepney and 3-14 against Hull Congos. When County Hall Wakefield visited the Pleasure Grounds, he demolished them with 7-29, though this was neither enough to engineer victory nor satisfy Spectator. County Hall's meagre 99 was still too many for Goole who replied with 88 (Jeeves bowled by a shooter for seven) and Jeeves's fine bowling did not elicit comment from the reporter who simply sniped that "Goole placed on the field the poorest side that has yet represented them".

If their batting was unreliable, there was also room for improvement in their powers of organisation. On 12 July the men from Sleepy Hollow were denied victory at Swanland Manor after running out of time in the quest for wickets. They had only themselves to blame.

"Owing to alterations to the train services," reported the paper, "and the fact that the secretary had not possessed himself of a penny diary, the team did not arrive at their destination until a somewhat late hour. Some, lucky enough to obtain a compartment, changed in the train. How the others envied them as they toiled up the hill to Swanland. The unlucky ones doffed hats and collars – and nothing else – but weighed less in the park than at Ferriby station."

Jeeves made light of the inconvenience. After the late start, he hit 18 out of 98/7 then took four quick wickets. The home team were clinging on at 43/8 when the last vestige of light left the day.

Jeeves ended the season with 43 wickets at 8.4 runs each. Many of his victims were clean bowled, surprised as the ball gathered pace off the pitch. Jeeves was not burly and nor was he lightning fast but he sent the ball down on the brisk side of medium, so the extra zip gained after it pitched made him a lethal bowler.

5.

"Weeping and wailing and gnashing of teeth" – The ominous cognomen of Duck – Mr Baker's XI – The Gentlemen bat with broomsticks

DURING THE following year, 1907, with Goole first XI now captained by teacher William Appleyard, Jeeves's reputation continued to grow but his ego did not. He just loved playing cricket and was equally at home representing the first team against arch-rivals or the Grasshoppers on a village green.

He did not play in the opening match of the season at Doncaster Plant Works but was back for the visit to Beverley on 11 May. It was a day of unseasonably scorching sun, under which Goole's team suffered at the whim of a home captain who took umbrage at their late arrival.

Again, they had trouble with the trains. It was a mishap which could happen to anyone who depended upon public transport, but Beverley's skipper showed no empathy. He punished them severely for their tardiness by allowing his team to bat on – and on and on. The ordeal of the Goole fielders at least gave Spectator the chance to wax lyrical – and he was at his most lyrical.

"Compared with the previous week, last Saturday's weather was extremely welcome. Our grandmothers' maxim 'Ne'er change a clout till May be out' was somewhat unsatisfying. In fact, the sun was so absurdly generous that one felt like casting anything rendered not strictly necessary by the police regulations. It was hot. So, by the way, was the Beverley team, in more ways than one.

"Probably the fixture with the Minster Men is the most ambitious on the Goole Town programme, for it is only a year or two since the Beverley men had regular fixtures with the Hull First XI. Unfortunately, the mighty have fallen, to some extent.

"The Goole team which took the journey on Saturday was a fairly good one on paper. Unhappily, there was no chance of testing its capabilities except in the bowling and fielding departments.

"To begin somewhere near the commencement, the Goole men had the privilege of steaming into the Hull station as the Beverley train was departing. Naturally there was weeping and wailing and gnashing of teeth. This was intensified later when the team arrived on the ground and found that there was only time for three hours' play. To aggravate matters, the Goole captain lost the toss – almost a penal offence on a hot day.

"Of the subsequent proceedings much might be said were the libel laws a little more elastic. To put it gently, the Beverley captain was so incensed with the railway company for their unpunctuality that he promptly decided to penalise the Goole team. He therefore took up a position on the refreshment side of the ground – in itself an unfriendly act on such a thirsty day – and complacently watched his batsmen help themselves to runs. It may be added that they did this on the slightest provocation. The early dismissal of Mitchell flattered to deceive, and the subsequent eviction of Cooper was merely a device to lure the Goole men to disaster. Davis and Handley took full advantage of a splendid wicket and carted the ball to the four corners of the earth.

"This went on with the utmost regularity despite the fine bowling of Jeeves and Horsnell, and some good groundfielding by the Goole men. At intervals the Minster clock intimated the passing hour, but nothing interfered with the serenity of the Beverley captain. Maintaining his position near the refreshment tent, the chiming of quarters, half-hours and hours disturbed him not. He had arranged to draw stumps at six o'clock and evidently he did not care whose stumps were drawn so long as he was not required to vacate the shade of the sheltering, etc.

"Close on half-past five, however, some sportsmanlike feeling – probably hitherto dormant, or newly-born – agitated his more or less manly bosom. It struck him that, after all, it was hardly the fault of the Goole team that the train was late. Overcome with remorse, he declared his innings closed, and generously allowed Goole to go in and riot for a whole half-hour. His reward may not be of this world, but it is more or less certain later on.

"Goole started badly and never seemed likely to get the 170 runs required within the half-hour. To commence with, one of the bowlers rejoiced in the name of Wilde, and the other bore the ominous cognomen of Duck. Goole therefore retired within their defences, and refused to be comforted. They even declined to get runs when the ball was clear away. This, I am inclined to think, was bad policy. If the Beverlonians were dead to all sportsmanship, the visitors were hardly doing the right thing in following a bad example. However, the Goole score stopped short at 13 for the loss of three wickets.

"It could not be called a particularly lively day's cricket, but there were compensations. Apart from the utter unselfishness of the Beverley men, the outstanding feature was the fielding of the Goole team. Appleyard brought off a really good catch in the long field. He watched the ball carefully for the whole of the fortnight during which it appeared to remain in the air and, after a wrestling match with a sub who was also after the catch, the Goole captain pouched the ball as if he would never, never let it go. It might, however, be just as well to remind the Goole men that the wicket-keeper prefers to have the ball thrown in to within a couple of yards of his hands when possible. Last Saturday, and the week before, the stumper had quite a warm time running after the ball. It should be remembered that a wicket-keeper, if he be a wicket-keeper, would just as soon the fieldsmen threw the ball at his nose as anywhere else."

Goole's reply to Beverley's 169/3 amounted to a bizarre 13/3. It was an afternoon during which tolerance and generosity of spirit were in short supply but if that match was ill-tempered and unsatisfactory, Jeeves soon figured in four which exuded the simple joy of cricket. The opposition: Adlingfleet, Luddington, The Ladies and Mr Baker's XI.

On Whit Monday, an informal game at the Pleasure Grounds saw Goole face Mr Baker's XI. It was an afternoon of low scoring and high hospitality. After Goole made 36, Mr Baker's XI replied with 31. Jeeves took two wickets while Petty took eight for…something. Spectator admitted: "I can't say for how many as the scorer was so busy writing 'bowled Petty' and digesting his lunch that he had no time to keep the analysis."

A Wednesday evening at the Pleasure Grounds then brought an enthralling tussle between the Ladies and Gentlemen. In Edwardian England, many men still regarded the roles of women in cricket firmly as those of decorative spectator or preparer of tea and the chaps somewhat condescendingly bowled left-handed and batted with broomsticks.

The Suffragette movement, at its height in its courageous pursuit of women's rights, might have baulked at that gesture but The Ladies of Goole played a straight bat and totalled 35 (Miss J. Hunter 19) before bowling out the Gents for 25. All very civilised – and around the corner were those exquisite afternoons at Adlingfleet and Luddington. Meanwhile, 5 July brought a happy event at 72 Manuel Street. At the age of 37, Nancy Jeeves gave birth to a fourth son, Harold. After a 17-year wait, Percy had a younger brother.

6.

A wrecked wicket – The 1880 Wild Birds Act – Jeeves ponders his future – Doncaster Plant Works

T HE CAREFREE fun of a game against Mr Baker's XI was a pleasant enough way to pass the time but Percy Jeeves was a cricketer of serious talent. And, to the delight of his team-mates, he showed his abilities to the full when the cricket was taken seriously – or far too seriously.

Hull Wilberforce's next visit to the Pleasure Grounds was a rancorous affair in which tempers became frayed. Young Jeeves simply let his cricket do the talking.

After Goole made 140 (Jeeves 35, Dr Dooley 38), the visitors disagreed with some umpiring decisions early in their reply, so simply ignored them. Two of their top-order batsmen were adjudged out, caught off Jeeves, but stood their ground. Wilberforce's best batsman, Wilson, was then bowled by Horsnell but refused to leave the crease after the non-striker insisted to him that the ball had missed the stumps and rebounded on to them off the pads of wicketkeeper Latham. Wilson would not go.

Held in contempt by the fielding team now, in the next over, Wilson ran a single and went down to face Jeeves. In the circumstances, with danders up, the batsman probably expected his young opponent to let him have the fastest ball he had got. Instead, down came a beautifully-disguised slower delivery which foxed the batsman completely. He swished and missed but, to howls of anguish from the fielders, the ball missed off stump by an inch. Wilson survived again.

Not for long. The next ball was the fastest of the day and sent two stumps flying.

"The batsman never saw anything but a wrecked wicket," reported a triumphant Spectator, "and as Latham was contemplating the wreckage with undisguised satisfaction from a three-yard distance, there could be no doubt about it."

That was one of four wickets for Jeeves, who led his team-mates back into the pavilion after Wilberforce were all out for 94, beaten by 46 runs. Jeeves continued to tower above his modestly-talented team-mates. On 15 August he hit 54 (retired) for Goole Thursday against Goole Police. Two days later, for the seconds at Saltmarshe, he took 5-10 to rattle the home side all out for 25. The visitors scraped home with 26 thanks, in part, to a Jeeves double-act, Percy scoring five from number three and elder brother Alick, a spin bowler who usually played for Goole Locomotives, six from number nine.

In the final game of the season, against a Hull XI at Anlaby Road, Percy was unwell and managed just one run and no wickets. But he did briefly play in front of the biggest crowd of his life so far. During half-time in Hull City's 2-0 victory over Barnsley in the Football League Division Two match on the neighbouring field, the crowd watching the cricket rose over 3,000.

Jeeves ended the season top of the Goole first XI bowling averages with figures that were remarkable even considering the poor batting wickets. He bowled 155.5 overs with 37 maidens and took 55 wickets for 323 runs, at an average of 5.87. His exceptional talent clearly belonged far above the gregarious but ramshackle confines of Goole.

During the winter, Jeeves took on the laborious duties of an office-boy at hardware store H. Williamson & Co. The prospect of a long-term future there was uninspiring, as was that of a life on the railways. The latter was likelier as railway work often passed through generations of families and Edwin was already planning to bring his boys into the fold. But was that what Percy wanted?

The days of 23 and 24 December brought thick fog upon Goole and a two-shillings fine for Mary Ann Shaw, of Pollington, for possessing two thrushes in contravention of the 1880 Wild Birds Act. Christmas Day dawned clear and bright. At the town's workhouse, the occupants looked forward to the rare treat of tucking into roast beef followed by plum pudding in rum sauce. At 72 Manuel Street, Percy Jeeves pondered his future.

The 1908 cricket season opened in the Goole area on 18 April when Creosote Works beat Blacktoft by 41 runs and Gilberdyke squeezed home by three runs in a thriller against Hull Neptune-street.

The previous day, Jeeves had been in action at the Pleasure Grounds but with pig's bladder rather than crimson rambler. He was in Swinefleet's defence for a Good Friday morning friendly against Goole Town Reserves and it was quite a match. With the wind at their backs, Town were 5-0 up at half-time ("Jeeves was stretched", reported the paper) then missed a penalty which would have made it 6-0 before Swinefleet fought back to finally lose 5-4.

Three days later, on Easter Monday, W.G. Grace, aged 59, began his last first-class appearance, for the Gentlemen of England against Surrey at The Oval, and it snowed.

Goole CC opened their season at Selby a fortnight later and Jeeves began as if he had no time to lose. He took six wickets, all bowled, in four overs and was "practically unplayable". A week later, a strong Hull XI visited the Pleasure Grounds and was blown away as Jeeves bowled his fastest yet. A succession of batsmen were left with bruised hands, arms and bodies while Jeeves also hit the stumps five times among his seven wickets.

After a six-for and a seven-for came an eight-for. At Doncaster Grammar School, Jeeves conceded 12 runs without taking a wicket then finished with 8-20, also top-scoring with 20 for good measure. Against Selby Londesborough, he "bowled with his accustomed excellence" for 16.2-5-30-6. He top-scored with 21 against Hull Church Institute then took five wickets to skittle them for 42.

Jeeves's all-round excellence, week after week, carried a team as struggling as it was disorganised. On 4 July, Goole failed to raise a side for the return match with Hull Church Institute. Again there were irritating gaps in the fixture list, one of which saw Jeeves turn out for the second XI against Thorne Brewery, a game in which his popularity was clear from the warmth shown by his opponents. On a lovely day at the Pleasure Grounds, Jeeves, the ace bowler in the area, was not brought on until very late and then every ball he bowled was greeted with ironic cheers by the brewery lads. He took the teasing with a smile and a wave.

Goole won their last match of the season, at home to Swanland Manor, by 79 runs. Percy Jeeves won it almost single-handedly, scoring 61 and taking 7-16. As he opened the football season in Swinefleet's defence in a 1-1 draw with Snaith, in cricket terms, he had clearly outgrown the Sleepy Hollow.

Jeeves would be 20 years old the following March. Ahead of him lay only a life of drudgery on the railway docks alleviated by some cricket at weekends. Edwin now had all his adult sons fixed up on the railways:

Thomas as a station clerk, Alick an engine stoker and Percy a dock labourer. But Percy had a special talent.

Goole firsts opened their 1909 season on 1 May with an away match at Doncaster Plant Works. They were thrashed and, much to the disgust of Spectator, omitted to send details to the newspaper. "Goole, we are told, could only compile 20," he reported, "while the Doncaster men slogged the Goole bowling about for something like 184 runs for the loss of four wickets – and this despite the fact the visitors had the assistance of Percy Jeeves."

It was the last time they were to have such assistance. Jeeves had been engaged as a professional cricketer.

7.

Athletic News – Professional at Hawes – Trial for Yorkshire – R.V. Ryder cuts himself shaving

P ERCY JEEVES was destined to play with and against the great figures of cricket's Golden Age. Even in an era teeming with stars, his cricket skills would shine. Distinguished judges, including England captain 'Plum' Warner, would predict a golden future for him.

Alongside his sporting prowess, meanwhile, Jeeves's immaculate conduct and appearance would leave an enduring legacy. The writer P.G. Wodehouse would apply Jeeves's name to a character who would become one of the great creations of English literature. The word 'Jeeves' was to become forever embedded in a nation's vernacular and consciousness. And none of this would have happened if a Birmingham businessman, on holiday in Wensleydale in 1910, had not cut himself shaving.

Like many sports-mad young men in 1909, Percy Jeeves was an avid reader of *Athletic News*. The weekly magazine featured interviews, reports and scores and, though largely devoted to football, also covered other sports, including cricket. Among its more than 100,000 readers were three young men at 72 Manuel Street, Goole, and an edition early in 1909 contained an advertisement which caught their attention. The ad was from Hawes Cricket Club, set in the magnificent countryside of North Yorkshire.

A small, elegant town in the Ure valley in Wensleydale, Hawes was a magnet for walkers while its indigenous people mostly farmed (the town was the home of Wensleydale cheese) or worked in the two mills. Like any self-respecting Yorkshire town or village, it had a cricket field – and it was a delight. Hawes Cricket Club nestled beside the river, overlooked by the rolling slopes of Abbotside Common. It was a heavenly place to play England's summer sport. So it should have been – it was purpose-built by order of a cricket fanatic.

Hawes Cricket Club was forged from the passion and financial clout of one man, Hugh Arden Crallan. Educated at Sutton Valence School in Kent and then Cambridge University, Crallan worked as a teacher until 1906 when, aged 39, he inherited a fortune following the death of a cousin. Suddenly, Crallan was free to follow the life of landed gentry. He engaged renowned London architect Percy Morley Horder to design a country house for him and, in 1908, on a hillside overlooking Hawes, The Stone House was built in fine art-and-crafts style.

Crallan's inheritance enabled him to fully indulge his two sporting passions; cricket and horse racing. Half a mile downhill towards the town, he laid out a cricket field, its tiny pavilion and undulating outfield just visible through the treetops from the house's tall front windows. Hawes Cricket Club was – and remains – a five-minute stroll from The Stone House one way and two minutes, across the little humped-back bridge over the river, from the centre of town the other.

Known locally as a "schoolmaster and idealist", Crallan loved to entertain. Friends from Cambridge and London frequently enjoyed his hospitality and central to that, in the summer, was cricket. His passion for the sport was immense, albeit not matched by ability. While an eager guest in matches arranged by fellow landowners, he rarely excelled. On 9 June 1893, guesting for Barnard Castle against Durham Club & Ground at Balliol Street, Crallan top-scored with 40 in a two-wicket victory. But invariably he was no more than an enthusiastic bit-part player. More typical was his input, two years later, for W.H. Whitwell's Durham County XI against F. Stobart's Burnmoor District XI in a match to celebrate the opening of Burnmoor Cricket Club's new £220 pavilion. Crallan scored seven and did not bowl in a seven-wicket defeat.

Crallan poured his passion for the sport into Hawes CC. He formed the club, laid out the ground, assembled the team and loved it when they won. With that in mind, in 1909, he decided to hire a professional. *Athletic News* was his chosen medium, in went the advertisement and, 93 miles from the rolling fields of The Stone House estate, in the tight, urban terracing of Manuel Street, Percy Jeeves, having just embarked upon a job labouring in the railway docks, took note. Here, perhaps, was a way to exploit his talent. He wrote out an application.

Jeeves was soon stepping off a train at Hawes. From the station, the young interviewee, in best garb and carrying his cricket kit, crossed the river bridge, passed the field that he hoped to soon tend and play upon, and pressed on up the lane to The Stone House. Jeeves interviewed well. Just as importantly, down on the cricket field, he played well. The perfect applicant, he was duly hired. Jeeves was appointed to work as a gardener on the estate, maintain the cricket field and play for the team as a professional. Liberated from the prospect of a life on the grimy railways, he left home to earn a living amid the open air of the dales.

Crallan was delighted by his recruit. Hugh and wife Edith had no children. At 42, fatherhood had passed him by but he took to Percy like father to son. Diligent, likeable and modest, Jeeves was easy to love but also possessed the cricket talent which Crallan craved. In his first season with Hawes, their new professional took 73 wickets at 5.3 each. He also scored plenty of runs, including 77 against Leyburn, and guested occasionally for other clubs. Bedale benefited most when, loaned out to them, he struck 102 against Thirsk.

Jeeves started the following season, 1910, in fine style with runs and wickets at home to Pendle Nomads. His three-figure score with the bat brought him a nice little earner, reported the 21 May edition of the *Darlington and Stockton Times*:

> "The Hawes Cricket Club opened their season on Whit-Monday, their opponents being the Pendle Nomads from Clitheroe. The home side declared their innings closed at 205 for seven wickets, and then dismissed their opponents for the small score of 24. Jeeves (108), J.E. Osborne (50) and H.A. Crallan (29 not out) made the runs for Hawes, and the Nomads fell before Jeeves (four wickets for six runs) and H.A. Crallan (six wickets for 18 runs). In appreciation of Jeeves's innings the sum of 30s was presented to him by the players and spectators."

Jeeves followed up one century with another, 109 as a guest for Bedale against York Trinity. He continued to demolish all comers in country house and village cricket with a verve which persuaded the well-connected Crallan to arrange a trial for him with Yorkshire County Cricket Club.

One of the county game's founding fathers, Yorkshire boasted a formidable team, including pillars of the England team Wilfred Rhodes and George Hirst, under the captaincy of the formidable Lord Hawke. They had won the county championship eight times in 16 years, including five times in the last ten, and the team was a source of fierce pride to the county. To be taken on to Yorkshire's staff was the stuff of only the wildest dreams for most young players but Crallan knew that Jeeves had a chance.

The landowner accompanied his young protégé to Harrogate where the trials were supervised by Gerry Weigall. A Cambridge blue who had played for Kent as an amateur, Weigall was a stickler for orthodox batting. His 6,866 first-class runs (at the modest average of 19.39) had been accumulated slowly and most effectively in rearguard actions. He was a stone-waller. And Jeeves's cavalier style of batting was anathema to Weigall.

As weeks passed with no word from the county club, Jeeves tended the estate at The Stone House and suspected that his chance in county cricket had come and gone. He never heard from Yorkshire again but continued to shine for Hawes until fate took a hand – courtesy of a clumsy hand.

Rowland Vint Ryder, secretary of Warwickshire County Cricket Club, visited the dales on holiday. Ryder was Yorkshire-born, at Wetherby, but had long been the administrative powerhouse behind Warwickshire. He joined the county aged 23 in 1896 as assistant secretary and quickly became secretary. In 1902, he organised Edgbaston's inaugural Test match almost single-handed. Eight years later, Ryder was responsible for all Warwickshire's back-room operations, including player recruitment.

In 1995, Ryder's son, also named Rowland, reported in his book of personal reminiscences, *Cricket Calling*, an amazing turn of events.

"In the late summer of 1910 my father, then Warwickshire secretary, was on a walking holiday in his native Yorkshire and stayed one night in the village of Hawes," recalled Ryder junior. "Using his murderous, cut-throat razor, he had mistimed a stroke while shaving; a visit to the local doctor was necessary. The doctor, having dealt with the cut, prescribed a visit to the afternoon's cricket match and here, on the lovely ground at Hawes, my father saw a young cricketer whose effortless grace as a bowler told something of his potential.

"At the end of the innings, he said to him: 'How would you like to play for Warwickshire?'"

Jeeves was later to offer a more prosaic version of events but, whatever the precise detail, an outrageous twist of fortune had presented him with a pathway into county cricket after all. If Ryder's hand had been steadier, he would have passed upon his way and Percy Jeeves would have remained a gardener. Similarly, had the doctor harboured no interest in cricket, he would have come up with a different suggestion for how Warwickshire's wounded secretary should spend his afternoon.

Instead, a thrilled Crallan added a ringing endorsement of Jeeves's character in a reference for the benefit of Ryder. The young man was "absolutely steady and reliable", he wrote. "He has given great satisfaction…the sole reason for his leaving is that he is worth far more than we can afford to pay him."

Crallan also wrote to Jeeves, who had returned to Goole for the winter, to urge him not to let this opportunity pass by and to send to the Warwickshire secretary a list of his exploits during the 1910 season (he scored three centuries and took 69 wickets at seven runs each), along with the relevant press cuttings.

Ryder was convinced. Warwickshire had endured several modest seasons and their bowling reserves were thin, so to pluck a player of such potential out of the hills of Wensleydale appeared a godsend. The secretary put the necessary procedures in motion and at a meeting of Warwickshire's general committee, at the Colonnade Hotel, Birmingham, on 27 October 1910: "It was decided to offer P. Jeeves of Goole an engagement for 20 weeks at 30 shillings, Yorkshire having consented."

A written offer of a professional contract for the 1911 season soon landed at 72 Manuel Street. Less than two years after playing his last game for Goole, Jeeves bade a fond farewell to Hawes and travelled south for the first time, to Birmingham.

8.

Ground duties at Edgbaston – S. Blanks becomes the first – Jeeves bowls F.R. Foster – A toast is drunk to 'The Press'

PERCY JEEVES'S entry into county cricket could not be immed-iate. A player had to reside in a county for two years to be elig-ible to play in the championship, so the new recruit spent 1911 settling into Birmingham and working around Warwickshire's Edgbaston ground under long-serving groundsman John Bates.

"The first year I did not get much match cricket and accomplished nothing out of the ordinary," Jeeves later recalled. He was, though, an onlooker to a success which was quite extraordinary.

Warwickshire's team approached the 1911 season in a dishevelled state. Since hurrying to first-class status in 1894, only 12 years after formation, and hosting their first Ashes test only eight years later, the club had lost momentum. In 1908 and 1909 they finished 12th of the 16 counties. In 1910, they dropped to 14th. Hopes for 1911 were far from high.

Under the reluctant captaincy of Charles Cowan, an officer in the navy and moderate cricketer who played for Warwickshire only occasionally, they began the season in wretched fashion with an innings defeat to Surrey at The Oval. That humiliation, in which Cowan bagged a pair, convinced the club's committee to beg brilliant all-rounder Frank Foster to take the captaincy. In January, just before his 22nd birthday, the maverick Foster had announced his retirement to concentrate on the family clothing firm in Digbeth. But after the

Surrey debacle, lobbied by his father John (a committee member), Frank reconsidered.

The effect was immediate and spectacular. In Foster's first match in charge, Warwickshire beat a powerful Lancashire side by 137 runs at Old Trafford. An immediate sign that Foster's captaincy was touched by inspiration came with the dismissal of the great Johnny Tyldesley. The right-hander was a linchpin of England's top order and a habitual plunderer of the Bears, averaging over 100 against them. He advanced smoothly to 13 in Lancashire's first innings and the home supporters sat back ready to enjoy another Tyldesley ton when, to widespread incredulity, Foster threw the ball to Jack Parsons, a young batsman who hardly ever bowled. The last ball of Parsons's first over was an appalling leg-side offering which Tyldesley, in his confusion as to whether to hit it for four or six, contrived to edge to Ernest 'Tiger' Smith behind the stumps.

Under Foster, Warwickshire went on to win 13 of 19 matches, culminating in a heavy victory over Northamptonshire at Northampton in the last game to clinch the championship for the first time. Foster led the way with bat (1,383 runs), ball (116 wickets) and sheer force of personality. Always positive, he led from the front while instilling great togetherness among a disparate group. Old and young, amateur and professional, local and imported, they pulled together to bring the title to Edgbaston. It was the first time any county outside the Big Six – Surrey, Yorkshire, Lancashire, Middlesex. Nottinghamshire and Kent – had won the championship. A stunning achievement.

In this momentous year did Percy Jeeves arrive at Warwickshire but, busy on ground duties and as a net-bowler for the amateurs, he played little serious cricket. In May he turned out in a couple of games for Wednesbury, against Forest of Arden and Erdington, but as the season deepened, duties at Edgbaston kept him occupied on most Saturdays.

His first appearance as a player on the Edgbaston turf arrived on a Monday and a Tuesday, 10 and 11 July, in a pair of friendlies for Warwickshire Club & Ground. In the annual match against Sixteen of Parks Association, the visitors batted first and, opening the bowling, Jeeves quickly dismissed the openers. S. Blanks, a parks official lost in the mists of time, became his first victim for the Bears. The Parks Association totalled 254 thanks largely to B. Barrett's unbeaten 70 from number 14 and Club & Ground replied with 183 for six, Jeeves scoring 32 batting at number three.

Next day, Fifteen of the Suburban League were the opposition and Jeeves took 4-18 and scored 86 not out. Further success came his way when Warwickshire second XI played a two-day game against Worcestershire at New Road. Jeeves took 16-8-25-5 and 14-4-33-1 in a nine-wicket win.

As the first team, watched by crowds of more than 10,000, charged towards the championship, on 22 and 23 August came a chance for Jeeves to shine in the annual Amateurs v Professionals two-day match at Edgbaston.

The amateurs were led by Foster and included talented batsman Reginald Pridmore (who had played hockey for England at the 1908 Olympics) and promising youngsters Eric Crockford and Horace Venn.

The professionals, among whom Jeeves lined up, consisted of the nucleus of the first XI – seasoned batsmen Septimus Kinneir, Billy Quaife and Crowther Charlesworth, wicketkeeper Tiger Smith, fast bowler Frank Field and medium-pacer Sydney Santall.

These were the men whom Jeeves aspired to join in the ranks of the first team and straight away he showed them his worth. He set the Professionals on the way to a five-wicket victory with 4-29, his victims including Foster and Pridmore. He also showed aptitude in the slips with three catches off Santall as the veteran took 6-45 in the second innings.

In September, Warwickshire were crowned champions for the first time and great were the celebrations at a lavish dinner in the Grosvenor Room of the Grand Hotel in Birmingham. The Earl of Warwick presided over a guest list including Lord Hawke, Lord Willoughby de Broke and the mayors of Birmingham, Aston, Leamington Spa, Stratford-upon-Avon, Nuneaton and Chichester. A telegram was read out from a company of the Royal Warwickshire Regiment, stationed in India. A toast was drunk to "The Press".

Gloucestershire and England batsman Gilbert Jessop addressed the gathering. "What Warwickshire's bowling lacked in quantity," he said, "it more than made up for in quality." It was certainly true that, assisted by hard wickets in a hot, dry summer, Frank Foster and Frank Field had vanquished all before them, but there was room for another seam bowler in the attack.

Jeeves's move south, it seemed, was a timely one.

His first season with Warwickshire had been frustratingly slight on the field but he still had plenty to write home about to Edwin and Nancy, still living in Manuel Street, and to report to Hugh Crallan at

The Stone House. On 8 September, Warwickshire secretary Ryder sat at his great oak desk in his office in the pavilion and composed a letter:

"Dear Jeeves, I am instructed by my committee to offer you an engagement for 12 months from August 26th at 62 for the year, payable as follows – £1 per week for the winter (32 weeks), 30/ per week for the summer (20 weeks), the understanding being that if you can find suitable employment you are to accept it for the winter pay. We shall arrange for you to play regularly for a league team on Saturday afternoons, but there will be no extra pay for these matches. The total amount payable to you during the year being £62. In mid-week matches for which you may be engaged (other than Club & Ground matches) you will be paid the usual rate: Viz 15/6. Our object in making this offer is of course to give you the opportunity of qualifying for the county. Your early reply will oblige."

It is safe to say that the back-dated offer received an early reply.

9.

The *Titanic* sinks – Jeeves shines for Moseley – West Bromwich Albion right-half George Baddeley is carried shoulder-high from the field – "The young Yorkshireman is to be heartily congratulated."

ALTHOUGH JEEVES would still not be qualified to play in the County Championship in 1912, he could look forward to his first competitive cricket as he spent the winter at right-back for Stirchfield Co-operatives in the Birmingham Wednesday League.

He was allocated to Moseley as their professional in the Birmingham League, a structure of high quality and intense competition. That would supply his biggest test yet but even more alluring was the prospect of two Warwickshire first-team matches for which he would be eligible. Australia and South Africa were due to tour England for a triangular Test tournament and both would play a three-day match at Edgbaston.

The club approached the 1912 season amid great excitement. On the back of the championship triumph, Warwickshire had recruited more than 500 new members and recorded a rare profit. Jeeves, meanwhile, continued to settle in the Second City. He took lodgings in the home of 62-year-old widow Martha Austin at 57 Stratford Place, at the city centre end of Stratford Road. Martha had three children – Annie, Henry and George – still living at home but boosted the household income by taking in a lodger. Before Jeeves arrived, it was Alfred Nightingale, a 43-year-old chamois leather dresser from Battersea.

George, the youngest sibling at the age of 21, worked at Warwickshire County Cricket Club as a clerk. He was soon to be formally appointed the Bears' first-team scorer, a duty hitherto allocated to whoever happened to be available on the day. George would become a close pal of Jeeves. His sister Annie, who worked as a brassfounder's order clerk and, at 34, was 11 years older than Percy, closer still.

Jeeves also befriended fellow young players Harold and Len Bates, sons of groundsman John. He worked hard, practised hard and learned all he could. Some fine mentors were there to impart advice; the mighty Frank Foster, gentle giant Frank Field, the veteran Sydney Santall and avuncular Crowther Charlesworth. Jeeves also briefly encountered a familiar and less judicious figure. Gerry Weigall, so unimpressed at Harrogate two years earlier, served a short-term coaching engagement at Edgbaston.

A fortnight before the 1912 season began, the nation was shocked by tragedy in the Atlantic. The *Birmingham Daily Post* reported: "NEW YORK, APRIL 15. The Titanic sank at 2.20 this morning. The steamer Olympic reports that the steamer Carpathia reached the Titanic's position at daybreak but found the boats and wreckage only…White Star officials admit that probably only 675 out of the 2,200 passengers on board have been saved."

Back in Birmingham, the Edgbaston Observatory reported the driest April on record. "The motor dust in the main roads in the Midlands has been terrible," reported the *Daily Post*. Perhaps Jeeves would have some nice, quick early-season pitches on which to bowl.

On 4 May, his scheduled debut in the Birmingham League for Moseley against Mitchells & Butlers at Edgbaston was rained off, but the weather was better five days later when he was loaned to the Birmingham University team to face Warwickshire Club & Ground. The Club & Ground side was virtually a full-strength first team, eager for practice and led by Foster. The Warwickshire captain had just returned from helping Johnny Douglas's side to record a crushing Ashes victory Down Under and was firmly established as one of English cricket's biggest and most flamboyant natural talents. Jeeves bowled him for five and, after Club & Ground scored 208/3, top-scored with 34 in the University's 115.

On 10 May, the papers reported that "Ernest Piggott will ride at Worcester today and tomorrow", a snippet of great interest to Hugh

Crallan but not to Jeeves who did not share his patron's passion for racing. Jeeves's thoughts were on his Moseley debut next day against Walsall at their recently-opened Gorway ground.

The game attracted "easily the largest crowd yet seen on the Walsall new ground, numbering over 2,000 on the unreserved part alone". Many spectators had come to see Foster who, the previous year, dismantled Walsall with 7-21 for Moseley. They were disappointed as this time, "feeling slightly unwell he did not bowl". Jeeves bowled though – and brilliantly. He hit the stumps of each of Walsall's top four batsmen and finished with 15-1-45-6. "At the onset, Jeeves, the new Moseley professional, carried all before him," reported the *Post*.

A week later, against Dudley at Edgbaston, Jeeves took 6-47 and struck an unbeaten 106. The *Post* correspondent, while lacking the descriptive whimsy of his counterpart on the *Goole Times*, was clearly impressed. "On an easy-paced wicket," he wrote, "the Dudley batsmen failed badly against the bowling of the young professional Jeeves and in slightly over an hour and a half were dismissed. Jeeves made the ball whip up from the pitch with plenty of life and his performance in taking 12 wickets in the first two league matches is one on which the young Yorkshireman is to be heartily congratulated."

Jeeves's chanceless 106 included 20 fours, five coming in one over. "Jeeves waited for the right ball to hit," reported the *Post*, "and, when he did so, showed fine driving power as well as a capable defence."

After 6-45 and 6-47 came 6-37 against West Bromwich Dartmouth at the Four Acres. Jeeves bowled S.H. Taylor with his fifth ball and hit the stumps another five times. After bowling Dartmouth out for 117, he was applauded from the field, although that ovation was bettered two hours later after Moseley were dismissed for 104. West Bromwich Albion right-half George Baddeley, who weeks earlier played for Albion against Barnsley in the FA Cup Final, took 6-23 and was carried shoulder-high from the field.

Jeeves's first three Birmingham League games had brought him 18 wickets at 7.16 each. Next he made a spot of batting history in a two-day Warwickshire second XI friendly against Northamptonshire. On the first day, in front of a crowd of around 1,200 at Edgbaston, he hit a six and ten fours as he struck 82 out of 223 before Northamptonshire closed on 275/5 against bowling which "with the exception of Jeeves appeared to lack sting". Next day the visitors cruised to a ten-wicket win but spectators in the pavilion witnessed something few had seen before – the ball struck clean over their heads into the road behind.

"Jeeves alone displayed any form with the bat," reported the *Post*. "Some of the brightest cricket of the day was shown by the young professional immediately after lunch when he drove Freeman into the pavilion and pulled Clarke to the leg for six. In the next over he drove Freeman clean out of the ground, the ball dropping into the Edgbaston Road adjoining the ground."

It was a shot which required astounding power and timing, especially taking into account the slenderness of the bats used in those days; mere shavings compared to the bludgeons with which many batsmen were to equip themselves in later years. By the time that archaic pavilion was finally demolished in 2010, only a handful of batsmen had managed such a blow.

10.

Herbert Hordern stays at home to concentrate on his dental practice – Jeeves make his debut against Australia – Kelleway edges behind – A perfect roar of applause

THE EDGBASTON pavilion was jam-packed a week later for the start of a three-day game against the Australians. The Aussies were in England for the first triangular Test tournament, an ill-fated enterprise which was never to be repeated. The brainchild of South African tycoon Abe Bailey, the series hit trouble before it began when Australia's 'Big Six' – Clem Hill, Victor Trumper, Warwick Armstrong, Albert Cotter, Vernon Ransford and Hanson Carter – pulled out following a pay dispute. With ace leg-spinner Herbert Hordern staying at home to concentrate on his dental practice, Australia were badly weakened. They were, though, still far superior to a South Africa side led by Englishman Frank Mitchell.

Yorkshire-born Mitchell played eight rugby and cricket Tests for England between 1895 and 1899 and served in the Yorkshire Dragoons in the Boer War but then remained in South Africa and ended up, courtesy of his friendship with Bailey, as that country's cricket captain. He returned to his former homeland at the head of a poor side. Captain Percy Sherwell and googly bowler Ernie Vogler did not travel following a legal wrangle with Bailey and the touring party included many untried players.

England, meanwhile, enjoying the fruit of the Golden Age, selected from arguably the greatest array of cricketers ever to grace one generation. Among them: Jack Hobbs, Frank Woolley, Gilbert Jessop, C.B. Fry, Plum Warner, Wilfred Rhodes, Tiger Smith, Jack Hearne, John Hitch, Reg Spooner and, most dynamic of all, Frank Foster and Sydney Barnes, who had just shared 66 wickets in the Ashes series in Australia.

The scintillating three-way duel which the organisers envisaged never materialised as rain ruined several Tests, crowds were poor and England won too easily. Neither touring side stretched the hosts but they did furnish Percy Jeeves with his first taste of first-class cricket.

Even a depleted Australian team was a huge attraction at Edgbaston and Warwickshire's supporters were optimistic that the champions would give the tourists a good game. The county shunned the unpopular policy adopted by others of raising admission from sixpence to a shilling for tour games and were rewarded with bumper crowds. At Goole, Jeeves played in front of a few hundred people; at Hawes, marquees full of minor gentry; and at Moseley, sometimes a couple of thousand. But as he watched Foster and Australia captain Sydney Gregory walk out to toss on a cloudy morning, the ground was abuzz with more than 10,000 people. It would be a test of the debutant's talent and also his temperament.

Australia had just trounced South Africa by an innings at Old Trafford in the opening match of the tournament. Leg-spinner Jimmy Matthews received a special cheer at Edgbaston, having made history at Manchester by taking a hat-trick in each innings, but the spectators were most excited to see Australia's batting. There was Charlie Macartney, unorthodox and destructive, who shared Foster's contempt for the unpunished bad ball. Warren Bardsley was a gifted left-hander who, three years earlier at The Oval, became the first player to score two centuries in a Test. Charles Kelleway's wicket, never sold cheap, was much-prized. Gregory first toured England in 1890 and had been part of every Australian tour since. His family were to Australian cricket what the Graces were to the English game.

Macartney, Bardsley, Kelleway, Gregory: a mighty quartet facing Jeeves, the young gun amongst the attack – Frank Foster, Frank Field, Sydney Santall and Willie Hands – which bowled Warwickshire to the championship. It was a mouth-watering backdrop to Percy Jeeves's introduction to first-class cricket.

His first act was to watch from the dressing room after Warwickshire won the toss and chose to bat. They advanced solidly as Kinneir (70) and Charlesworth (56) added 122. Quaife nurdled his way to 34 and Foster struck a breezy 29 (the captain "enjoyed half an hour's batting as only a young and enthusiastic cricketer can" reported the *Post*) but then Australia fought back. A gripping contest unfolded and when, at 245/6, Jeeves walked to the crease to join Moseley team-mate George Stephens, the ground was full of noise.

"The struggle for runs aroused the keenest possible interest amongst the big crowd, every run being cheered," said the *Post*. And the noisy atmosphere contributed to what happened next. After opening his account with a single, Jeeves chopped the ball to third man and set off again. An easy one was there but Stephens did not move. Perhaps the calls were lost in the din but Bardsley's throw was fast and accurate and, to the dismay of the crowd, Jeeves departed, run out for one. Most disappointed of all was Hugh Crallan who travelled from Hawes to watch his protégé despite suffering an attack of lumbago.

Warwickshire were 275 all out and, when the Australians batted after tea, the clouds darkened. Foster bowled Edgar Mayne without a run on the board but Claude Jennings and Macartney batted watchfully. Jeeves waited in the slips for a nod but Foster deployed himself, Field and Hands until the light closed in with Australia 80/1. It amounted to a quiet first day for Jeeves – one run and no bowling. But the next morning was to bring a thrilling glimpse into the future for Warwickshire's supporters: Foster and Jeeves operating in deadly tandem.

Australia added another 55 runs without further loss before Macartney, on 90, edged Foster to wicketkeeper Smith. Jennings fell the same way for 68 and, with Field proving expensive, the captain tried Hands, then Santall and even the spin of Billy Quaife, before turning to Jeeves.

Against mighty Australia, in front of a huge crowd, the nerveless youngster looked immediately at home. He dropped straight onto the right line and length and Kelleway, who had not played a false shot on his way to 17, was soon defeated by an off-cutter and edged to Smith. A notable maiden first-class scalp for the debutant.

With Foster deadly from one end and Jeeves imposing pressure at the other, Australia collapsed from 135/1 to 208/8 at lunch. Foster took five wickets in the morning session while his junior partner took just one but, beating the bat regularly, was equally impressive. The two bowlers were cheered from the field. The spectators liked the look of the figures on the little white scoreboard at the City End and also of this new fellow who could clearly bowl a bit. Their disappointment was great when rain set in during lunchtime and washed out play for the day.

Despite the saturated state of the field, Australia were keen to play on the final morning and, with the biggest crowd of the match present, a prompt start was made. Sid Emery and Harold Webster added 19 uncomfortable runs before Jeeves unleashed a break-back which shattered the former's wicket. Australia were 262 all out and the debutant had a highly creditable 14-3-35-2.

Eager to make a game of it, Foster then sent in the hitters. Stephens and Smith perished quickly and when Foster fell to a brilliant one-handed catch by Emery at mid-on, it was 63/4 and Jeeves went in. It was soon 64/5 as Kelleway gained his revenge with an away-swinger which Jeeves edged to perish for a duck.

Going for broke in poor light, Warwickshire made 102 to leave Australia 116 to win in just over a session. Foster and Field took up the attack amid a tumultuous atmosphere redolent of the Ashes Tests at the ground in 1902 and 1909. To thunderous cheers, Jennings edged Field. Australia: 1/1. Foster, striving too hard for pace, was expensive but Field was bang on target only for his fielders to let him down. Mayne was dropped by Charles Baker at point. The same batsman edged to slip and Hands fumbled, "both mistakes probably being the result of the prevailing excitement" suggested the *Post*.

Hands struck a big blow though – "There was a perfect roar of applause when Hands completely broke through Macartney's defence at 43. It was anybody's game now" – and the veteran Gregory went in at 43/3 with all results possible. But just as Australia's captain reached the crease, the heavens opened. A potentially wonderful climax to the match was washed away as spectators in the open stands hurried for cover and Jeeves, still to bowl in the innings, rounded off his debut with a sprint to the pavilion gate.

He had acquitted himself very well, which meant more cuttings to cull from the newspapers next day. Like so many young sportsmen, Jeeves collected the reports of his better days on the field and pasted them into a scrapbook. The first entry – an ageing report of his exploits with Alexandra Street Board School in Goole – was now getting more and more company in the book which, thanks to the diligence of Percy's younger brother Harold, still exists.

In 1980, Harold gave the scrapbook, along with two *Wisden Cricketers' Almanacks* which were owned by Percy, to author and collector David Frith, with whom they remain today.

11.

Middle stump a speciality – Seven Nondescripts score nought – Jeeves faces South Africa – Feeble batting, slack fielding, an attack without sting

WARWICKSHIRE'S HOPES of recording a historic victory over Australia may have been washed away but the debutant had made an excellent first impression. It came at the start of an interesting month for Percy Jeeves which began and ended against Australia and South Africa with, in between, games against Handsworth Wood, Warwick School, Kidderminster, Smethwick and Nondescripts.

Jeeves did not get on the field as Moseley v Handsworth Wood was trimmed to nine overs by rain but the weather improved for Warwickshire Club & Ground's Wednesday afternoon visit to Warwick School. Batting at five, Jeeves bagged a duck (caught by sixth-former Arthur Garrett off the bowling of the head of modern languages Thomas Bumpus) in the C&G's 147, but then bowled his team to a thrilling win.

Watched by hundreds of boys given the afternoon off, the Reverend John Day (school chaplain and head of English) was steering the school to victory until Jeeves, brought on late, bowled him for 82. Jeeves also bowled head of mathematics Charles Beechey for five, R.G. Hart (a groundsman) for one, Eric Pyne (son of the headmaster) for ten and Garrett for one. He took the last five wickets, hitting the stumps every time, to leave the school 146 all out and beaten by one run.

"Jeeves was put on," reported the school magazine *The Portcullis*, "and the remaining batsmen, more afraid of his reputation than of his actual bowling, allowed him to get rid of them for an additional 20 runs." Although the school lost the match, the boys cheered Jeeves off the field after a wonderful game of cricket.

Back with Moseley in the Birmingham League, Jeeves faced Kidderminster at Edgbaston. Batting at number three, between twins Frank and George Stephens, he scored 61 ("considering the forceful nature of his cricket there were few faulty strokes in his display" commented the *Post*) and then took 4-64 to set up an 89-run victory.

A week later at Smethwick, he was close to a very special hat-trick. After Moseley made 126 in front of "a capital crowd at the Harry Mitchell Park", Jeeves quickly uprooted Smethwick opener James Pigott's middle stump and, next ball, sent Bucknell's middle stump flying. He was denied a middle stump hat-trick by Burgoyne but it was becoming clear that a remarkably high proportion of this bowler's wickets involved rearranging the batsman's furniture.

Another Wednesday afternoon outing saw Jeeves guest for Dudley against Nondescripts at Edgbaston. He made 41 of his side's 226 before Nondescripts were all out for 25. Jeeves's input in the field was restricted to a catch to oust the second highest scorer, Johnson, for six, one of six wickets for C.H. Grimshaw. Seven Nondescripts lived down to their name with ducks. The next opponents were not so nondescript. South Africa.

The second tourist match of the season at Edgbaston lacked the lustre of the first. The South Africans had beaten Derbyshire, Surrey, Worcestershire, Cambridge University and South Wales but lost heavily in two Tests. They were beaten by an innings and 88 runs by Australia at Old Trafford and an innings and 62 runs by England at Lord's. In the latter match, Frank Foster and Sydney Barnes shared 19 wickets, including five each in the first innings to dismiss Mitchell's side for 58.

Rain was hindering the South Africans' search for form and they arrived in Birmingham early after the last day of their match against Middlesex at Lord's was curtailed. With a Test against England starting in Leeds two days after the Warwickshire game, their need for practice was great.

To deny the tourists practice against him, Foster did not play against them for his county, the captaincy passing to 23-year-old George

Stephens, an Edgbaston-born middle-order batsman and team-mate of Jeeves at Moseley. On a gloomy opening morning, the atmosphere in the ground contrasted vividly to that at Jeeves's debut a month earlier. Only 1,200 people paid for admission on the first day with less than half of those in at the start. The stay-aways were vindicated by a slow day's play after Warwickshire chose to bat.

"DULL BATTING BY THE COUNTY" announced the *Post* headline, though it was also a case of bad batting against a makeshift attack. Only stone-waller Septimus Kinneir showed the necessary patience on a rain-affected wicket. Eyebrows were raised when Mitchell asked Louis Stricker to purvey his occasional slows for the first time on the tour but he soon had Charlie Baker caught in the deep by 'Tip' Snooke, bringing in Jeeves to join Kinneir at 68/5. Jeeves "made two capital drives, on and off for threes" but reached only nine before attempting a big hit off Stricker and sending up a skier. The same bowler had Kinneir caught behind and finished with 3-13, figures which remained the best of a career which was to bring him only eight first-class victims in 60 games.

Warwickshire were 92 all out and, when South Africa started batting at 5.15pm, Stephens bizarrely denied Jeeves the new ball. He opened with Charlesworth (principally a batsman) and the ageing Santall and South Africa reached 60/3 before Jeeves and Hands were "afforded a long-deferred trial". The experienced Aubrey Faulkner, having scored 45 out of 67, soon took a liberty with a good-length ball from Jeeves and sent up a catch to Charlesworth. That was 70/4 but Stephens permitted Jeeves only four overs (4-0-12-1). Surrey-born left-hander Dave Nourse (a convert like Mitchell: he first went to South Africa as a 17-year-old drummer-boy with the West Riding Regiment) hurried to 41 by the close, at which South Africa were 131/5, 39 ahead. If rain stayed away, a two-day finish appeared certain.

A 1,000 crowd on the second day did not see Jeeves bowl again as South Africa advanced to 189 all out, for a lead of 97. At first, Warwickshire's second innings was as unimpressive as their first as they struggled against Pegler's medium pace and the left-arm spin of Claude Carter. They limped to 41/4 before Billy Quaife (63 in three hours) and Baker (a much brisker 50) added 85.

Jeeves went in at 126/5 and accompanied Quaife through to tea but, straight after the interval, was bowled by Pegler for 15. Warwickshire were 179 all out, leaving South Africa 83 to win and the tourists started batting at 6pm determined to finish it that night.

Again Stephens did not call upon Jeeves, even when opening bowlers Santall and Charlesworth were "freely hit". Play was extended to 7.10pm to get the game finished and the tourists won by six wickets.

Under-used by his captain and with his team outclassed in front of small crowds over two cold, grey days, Jeeves's second first-class game was underwhelming. The *Post* went hard at the wobbling county champions. "The majority of the men are palpably off-colour," the paper lamented. "In addition to much feeble batting, the attack has lost much of its sting while some of the fielding has been unusually slack, especially in picking up cleanly. Without the services of their captain F.R. Foster and with a pitch altogether unsuited to Field's bowling, the county team were handicapped."

Oozing potential, Jeeves was clearly a solution in waiting to the team's bowling problems. Rules were rules, though, and unfortunately for Warwickshire, after the two tourist matches he had to be banished back to Birmingham League duties to serve the rest of his qualification period.

12.

20 all out – Santall takes all ten against Samuel Talboys's XI – Jeeves fields for five minutes in the County Championship – The Birmingham League champions are routed

STRAIGHT AFTER facing South Africa, Percy Jeeves returned to club duty for Moseley's home game with Birmingham League leaders Walsall. Moseley were happy to be back at their Reddings home, having just sorted out a new lease, but did not have a happy day. They were flattened by the champions-elect.

After the visitors made 192 (Jeeves 18-1-51-1) Moseley reached 12 without loss then imploded to 20 all out. Fast bowler Gordon Hawley, having returned from holiday to play in the game, took 7-12, six of the runs conceded coming from one blow by Frank Stephens. Jeeves was bowled by veteran medium-pacer Billy Brammer for five. "Moseley's return to their old home at the Reddings has so far been attended with disastrous results," observed the *Post*. "It is evident the players will take time to get accustomed to the ground which has, in days gone by, been the scene of some exhilarating cricket."

On 8 July Jeeves was back at Edgbaston to play for Warwickshire Club & Ground against Eighteen of Parks Association. He took two wickets and two catches in the Parks Association's 119 and scored 18 as the match was tied. Two days later came a visit to Camp Hill School for WG Quaife's XI v Samuel Talboys's XI, a benefit match for Talboys, who had been coach and groundsman at the school for 16 years. Aged 39, Santall seized the chance to get among the wickets with 11.1-8-3-10 in Talboys's XI's 36 all out while Jeeves neither batted nor bowled.

Back in the Birmingham League Jeeves took four wickets for 68 to help his side to victory at Dudley before, on 19 July, came his first, very brief, experience of County Championship cricket. When Northamptonshire visited Edgbaston, the match sped along and the visitors ended the second day on the verge of defeat. Chasing 463 for victory, they were 158/9 in their second innings but, cricket being cricket, rather than finish the match, the teams played for the allotted amount of time and then promptly left the field. Everyone had to return next day for what could only be a matter of minutes, possibly seconds.

On the third morning, wicketkeeper Tiger Smith was injured so Charlie Baker took the gloves and Jeeves was called upon to field as a substitute. At half past 11, out he went with the Warwickshire team for the first time on championship business. That business was brisk. From the sixth ball of the day, Quaife had 'Fanny' Walden caught at short leg. Jeeves's first session of championship cricket lasted two minutes and was watched by almost no one.

The summer remained rain-affected but Jeeves continued to issue reminders that, come 1913, he would be a serious contender for regular first-team cricket. Against West Bromwich Dartmouth at Edgbaston he bowled through the innings for 16.3-1-46-6. When Aston Unity visited the Reddings, the saturated ground was unfit for play but a start was made as it was a benefit match for veteran professional Riley. In near darkness, with players barely able to keep their feet, Jeeves collected 33 with "spirited hitting". For Warwickshire C&G against Sutton Coldfield, he took the last three wickets, as so often, all bowled. When Sydney Santall's XI visited AW Barnes' XI at Lichfield he demolished the hosts with 7-19. But he saved his best until last.

On 31 August, in the final league game of season, Smethwick were skittled for 62 at The Reddings: Jeeves 14.2-7-17-6. On the same day, Walsall beat Handsworth Wood by six runs to clinch the Birmingham League title. Their achievement set up the inaugural Champions v Rest of League game, a week later. Unbeaten in the league all season, Walsall had a superb team – powerful, experienced and full of swagger. But Jeeves demolished them with a display of all-round brilliance.

The champions batted first and Len Taylor took guard. When E.J.A. Cook wrote *The Gorway Story* in 1958, the left-handed Taylor was still rated "probably the most brilliant batsman Walsall has ever produced" but his stumps were demolished by Jeeves's second ball. Jeeves then bowled Greaterex to have Walsall 14/2 and, "keeping a capital length", bowled captain Billy Preston and trapped Brammer lbw with successive balls. He bowled star all-rounder Clarence Eaton to make it 30/5 and when Norman Hewson, having counter-attacked for 20, lifted a catch to point, thoughts were turning towards a ten-for. That wasn't to be but Jeeves took 7-19 as Walsall, having carried all before them that season, were ignominiously all out for 48.

Jeeves had not finished. After the Rest of League's reply dipped to 34/4, he first played carefully to see his team to victory and then, batting on in the showpiece match, climbed into the champions' bowling for an unbeaten 74 (including two sixes, nine fours and a three) out of 172. It was a stunning all-round performance from the modest Yorkshireman.

Jeeves finished his first season in the Birmingham League placed third in the competition's bowling averages with 44 wickets at 10.48 runs each. He was 14th in the batting list with an average of 25.20 which was more impressive than the relatively low figure suggests. Runs were rarely easy to acquire on difficult, uncovered wickets and only seven batsmen in the league ended the season averaging over 30.

Jeeves's bowling figures of 150.2-17-461-44 were built by performances of consistently high quality but never more vividly was his talent displayed than on that sunlit September day in the dying embers of the 1912 season when his second delivery demolished the wicket of the classy Taylor. Jeeves and Taylor – two fit, happy, talented young sportsmen with towering futures. Nobody in the big, high-spirited crowd watching at Gorway had the faintest inkling that, within four years, both men would be dead.

13.

Cold and wet – The Guller wins the Chester Cup – Championship debut at Tipton Road – "Lifeless and depressing in the extreme"

PERCY JEEVES had everything to prove as the 1913 season approached. Was this young man, fished out of country house cricket in the Yorkshire Dales, good enough for the first-class game? County cricket featured the best players in the world and, in the Golden Age, it was to transpire, many of the best players ever. Could he compete?

The weeks leading up to the season were cold and wet. Jeeves was fit and ready thanks to regular duty in defence for Stirchley Co-operatives during the winter but, come April, many of his Warwickshire team-mates, aged nearer 40 than 30 and with sedentary winter jobs, badly needed outdoor practice. Day after day of rain made that impossible.

Hugh Crallan's horse, The Guller, won the Chester Gold Cup (and 2,550 sovereigns), triggering celebrations at The Stone House but Jeeves was not interested in racing. His concern, as his championship debut in the local derby against Worcestershire at Dudley drew near, was a lack of match practice. He was due to play for Warwickshire Club & Ground against Leicestershire at Edgbaston but the game was washed out, as was Moseley's Birmingham League opener at Smethwick.

At Lord's, the season's curtain-raiser between Middlesex and MCC was abandoned without a ball bowled. It was an unremittingly dreary spring and, to the dismay of Worcestershire, close to bankruptcy and desperate for bumper crowds for their neighbours' visit, the weather remained poor when the day of Jeeves's debut dawned. The morning of 12 May, Whit Monday, was miserable enough to keep all but the most determined spectators away from the Tipton Road ground beneath the ruins of Dudley Castle. After the home side chose to bat, it was a cold, damp arena on to which Percy Jeeves walked as a championship cricketer for the first time.

Despite poor light and rain in the air, play began on time at noon and Jeeves was straight into action. He opened the bowling but, with a wet ball in hand-numbing cold, to little effect. The players shivered through 80 minutes of play, Worcestershire moving to 77 without loss, before drizzle turned into downpour. Off they went – and off they stayed. Jeeves's first day as a championship cricketer was a chilly fragment. But on Tuesday the sun shone, more than 4,000 people attended and the debutant was among the wickets.

Worcestershire advanced to 208/6 with Bertie Stevens, on his home club ground, cheering the locals with some carefree drives on his way to 26. Then Jeeves was called back into the attack, Stevens drove at his first ball and a fast, swinging full-pitcher wrecked the stumps. His first championship victim secured, Jeeves quickly added his second as Richard Burrows fell lbw. After Ernie Bale edged to Septimus Kinneir in the slips, the newcomer finished with 11.4-4-29-3.

"Jeeves also distinguished himself," reported the *Post*, "by making the best catch of the day, off Field, which dismissed Australian all-rounder John Cuffe. It was made in the long field and in a particularly difficult position, having to turn while running in order to take the ball."

After Worcestershire were all out for 218, their supporters were delighted to see Warwickshire's rusty batsmen muster a meagre 142 in reply. Jeeves contributed only five runs to that total but the debutant kept his team safe from a surprise defeat on the final day. Needing quick runs in the morning, Worcestershire were stalled by Jeeves's 15-over spell which contained 12 maidens, with eight in a row. His 22-15-23-1 included the wicket of captain Henry Foster, the eldest of seven brothers who represented the county, whose middle stump was uprooted. That was a satisfying moment for Warwickshire because Foster had killed the game by delaying his declaration until he completed his half-century.

Set an impossible 269, Warwickshire responded with disdain. Frank Foster, who disliked his namesakes from across the county line, did not bother to bat while Stephens allowed the ball to hit his wicket, just as Keith Miller was famously to do at Southend 35 years later (as Australia piled up 720 in a day against Essex, Miller went in at 364/2, allowed his first ball to hit the stumps, muttered "Thank God that's over" and departed). Miller disliked cricket which lacked intensity and would no doubt have agreed with the *Post* reporter's description of the final day at Dudley as "lifeless and depressing in the extreme".

It was far from depressing for Jeeves though. His match figures of 33.4-19-52-4 represented a highly satisfactory baptism in championship cricket.

14.

"A most valuable addition to the team" – The disappearance of a donkey in Southampton – Jeeves dismisses the son of a friend of Charles Dickens – Mead bats brilliantly

TWO DAYS later came Percy Jeeves's championship home debut, against Leicestershire at Edgbaston – and this time he shone with bat and ball.

On the first day, Warwickshire struggled to 169/6 before Jeeves joined fellow youngster Jack Parsons at the crease. They added 60 – of which Jeeves's share was 46. "The most delightful batting was that of Jeeves whose spirited display was the best feature of the day," commented the *Post*.

After the Bears recovered to 282, Jeeves assured them a solid first-innings lead with 15.5-7-24-3 on the second day, dismissing veteran batsman Harry Whitehead, who had dug in for 46, and tail-enders John Shields and Alex Skelding. Already, Warwickshire's committee had seen enough. When Jeeves went into bat again just before the close, he was wearing his county cap, awarded during only his fourth first-class match.

Warwickshire ended the second day 434 in front with Jeeves on 15. Next morning he was stumped for 23 then obliterated Leicestershire's pursuit of 454. He dismissed Sam Coe, William Odell and William Shipman with alternate balls in an over, then had Shields caught by

Septimus Kinneir at cover-point and bowled last man Skelding. His 12.1-3-37-5 sealed a 271-run victory and a splendid home debut brought 69 runs and match figures of 28-10-61-8.

Jeeves, opined the *Post*, was "unquestionably a most valuable addition to the team". He had proved that he could trouble first-class opposition just as he used to torment the likes of County Hall Wakefield.

Percy Jeeves had always lived for cricket. Now he lived cricket. There was no time to digest his excellent start as Warwickshire played on 12 of the next 14 days. Against in-form Derbyshire at Derby he batted usefully for 19 and 36 but made little impact with the ball (1-48 and 0-23) in a seven-wicket defeat. Still, he topped the county's embryonic bowling averages for the season with 13 wickets at 14.15 as he embarked upon his first ever trip to the south of England for back-to-back games against Hampshire and Surrey.

The first two weeks of the season had been relentlessly grey but on Monday 26 May Warwickshire's players woke in Southampton to find the sun shining from a cloudless sky. Hampshire's Northlands Road home, its red-tiled pavilion sparkling, was a picture. Flowers filled the hanging baskets in the Ladies' Pavilion and the white scoreboard, considered the best in the country, gleamed after an early-morning wash. The outfield was lush green following all the rain and the pitch lovingly tended by groundstaff whose older members still, in quiet moments, pondered the mysterious disappearance of the groundsman's donkey back in 1889 (when even the offer of a ten-shilling reward failed to expedite the beast's return). With a good crowd, the setting merited a fine match. And that is what followed; a compelling contest featuring a great innings in a losing cause.

Many of Warwickshire's senior players – Frank Foster, Septimus Kinneir, Crowther Charlesworth, Frank Field, Sydney Santall – were still to find form and again, on the first day, it was young Jeeves who kept his team in the game. Foster chose to bat on a good wicket but the Bears managed only 260.

At 111/1 in reply, Hampshire were heading for a handsome lead but then Jeeves, as was his habit, struck immediately after coming on. Ernest Remnant, whose father, George, was a friend of Charles Dickens, edged a leg-cutter and Smith dropped the ball but kicked it up again and caught it. Alec Bowell, having hurried to 53, was deceived by a change of pace and spliced to Santall at mid-off, then George Brown edged behind. After three quick wickets for Jeeves, Hampshire closed on 136/4. Philip Mead was still there on 14, however. The left-hander's defence was considered the tightest in county cricket so he would take some dislodging in the morning.

Mead's technique was tested to its limits as Jeeves probed away, assisted by some early life in the wicket. The batsman added only two to his total before he edged but Kinneir grassed the chance at second slip. Unflustered, the young bowler persevered (putting the ball in the right areas, as it was to become known a century later) and Mead was beaten again and again. Then along came another perfect leg-cutter and, this time, the edge was held by Hands at third slip. One of the best batsmen of the day walked away, out for 25 and outplayed.

Despite Jeeves's 4-56, Hampshire led by 59 on first innings but then Warwickshire found some batting form. Smith hit Remnant over the pavilion in a lusty 57 while Foster, "brilliant in the extreme", blazed 111 in 115 minutes. The Bears ended the second day on 303/4 – 244 ahead. The match was perfectly set up for a great final day.

The sun was determined to witness all of this fascinating match and beamed down on Northlands Road on Wednesday morning as Warwickshire sought quick runs. Jeeves, six not out overnight, drove and glanced Brown for fours in a perky 28 before the visitors were all out for 389. At ten past one, Hampshire set off in pursuit of 331.

Jeeves soon surprised Bowell with bounce and bowled him off his wrist: 14/1. Remnant edged Foster into the slips: 21/2. Jimmy Stone sliced Jeeves to point: 41/3.

Field replaced Foster and had Brown caught in the slips: 48/4. Hampshire took lunch at 50/4. They were in trouble but their supporters still had hope; Mead was still there.

When a Foster yorker thudded into Newman's pads, it was 70/5 but Mead combined immaculate defence with severe punishment of anything loose to the delight of an enthralled 3,000 crowd. He enjoyed one slice of luck, on 35, when he edged Jeeves but Foster dropped the chance in the slips, then at last received some support as William Jephson and John Rutherford dug in.

The former knuckled down for 22. The latter was destined not to leave giant footprints upon cricket history (30 years later his obituary in *Wisden Cricketers' Almanack* stated, rather baldly, that "Rutherford J.S., who played for Hampshire in 1913, died on April 14, 1943") but defended doggedly to score four runs while 43 were added.

When Rutherford was castled by Jeeves (yet another start-of-spell wicket) and Foster bowled Arthur Jaques, the home side were 194/8 and the game looked up. But slow bowler Hamilton Haigh-Smith hung in there and, at tea, Mead was on 144 and the match was still alive.

In the final session, the ninth-wicket stand grew to 64, within 71 of victory before Mead, in search of his 28th four, drove at Hands. He connected sweetly but incipient applause for another boundary gave way to gasps of disbelief as the bowler clutched a brilliant, one-handed return catch. Mead stood in disbelief for a moment, then departed. In 190 minutes he had scored 170 out of 246 (his last 108 coming out of 124) and he left to a standing ovation in which Warwickshire's players participated.

Two overs later, Jack Moore edged Hands to Smith and Warwickshire had won a wonderful match by 64 runs. The figures of Jeeves (3-81) and (Foster 3-104) were bruised by Mead's brilliance but the all-rounders had inflicted enough early damage to set up victory. Jeeves had pocketed another seven wickets in the match and it was a happy team which headed from Northlands Road to the station to catch a London train. Waiting next morning: Surrey at The Oval.

15.

Quaife is barracked – Foster collides with a sideboard – The burden falls upon Jeeves – A ferocious new-ball spell

IT WAS a long way from the Victoria Pleasure Grounds in Goole to The Oval – and not just in miles. The humble plot where Percy Jeeves played as a boy had a small bandstand and a modest grandstand. The Oval boasted one of the finest pavilions in world cricket and seats on all sides. Goole CC's matches were conducted to a backdrop of din and stench from the docks. Surrey's players heard only the rumble of city traffic. The men of Sleepy Hollow were thrilled to middle the ball twice an over. Surrey had Jack Hobbs and Tom Hayward, considered by many to be the best opening pair cricket had ever seen, and numerous other star players.

The venue where Jeeves began his career in adult cricket was named after a monarch. The Oval's royal connection was direct. The ground reportedly owed its existence to the intervention of the Prince Consort, acting for Edward, Prince of Wales (later King Edward VII), who prevented the land being built upon before 10,000 turves were brought from Tooting Common to form a cricket field.

Since those turves were laid, the plot had become one of the world's foremost cricket stages. Home to one of the 'Big Six', its thousands of regular spectators enjoyed watching bowlers struggle against the great Hobbs and Hayward and batsmen fending off the bounce of John Hitch and groping at the taunting slows of Bill 'Razor' Smith. Those regulars were a partisan bunch who sometimes needed keeping in check. In 1889, 50 police officers, including three on horseback, patrolled the ground for the visit of Nottinghamshire while, more recently, plain-clothes policemen were appointed to eject anybody using "improper language". On and off the field, The Oval asked serious questions of visiting players. Percy Jeeves had adjusted adroitly to every challenge set before him so far. Here was the biggest.

On a grey morning beneath the gasometers, Warwickshire chose to bat, wobbled to 24/3 and then took the slow route out of trouble. Few batsmen could build walls of more impenetrable stone than Billy Quaife and he inched to a painstaking century. As Quaife plopped forward in defence time after time, he was loudly barracked but he had heard it all many times before. If anything, the abuse made the little man, 5ft 3in of unflappable defiance, all the more determined. He reached his ton after tea – and then retreated even further into his shell.

The barrackers ran through their repertoire – ironic cheering, slow hand-clapping, abuse – and were worn down into silence before Quaife was eventually run out for 124. More suffering followed for the crowd, though, as Jack Parsons scored just a single in 30 minutes, leaving everything outside off stump to more ironic cheers, on his way to 42. Only Jeeves's perky 39 lifted the mood, his "workmanlike methods making a strong appeal to the crowd".

After recovering to close the day on 325/9, Warwickshire were happy to arrive at the ground on Friday morning to find steam rising from the square after a night of heavy rain. "With sun scorching the ground," the *Post* reported, "the protecting mats laid on the wicket were still under water."

Warwickshire declared overnight to get straight at Surrey's batsmen but Hobbs and the hard-hitting Morice Bird (Hayward, now aged 42 and a little overweight in the twilight of his career, sometimes dropped down the order) punished the new ball for 50 in 27 minutes against Foster and Santall. The opening stand reached 72 before Jeeves was called upon and, in his first over at The Oval, he had Bird caught at square leg by Parsons. He also quickly removed Ernest Hayes and Hayward (batting at four) for nought. When Hobbs, having played with customary elegance for 88, sought his ninth four but edged to Charlesworth in the slips, Surrey were 174/4 and all the wickets had fallen to Jeeves.

Batting was not easy on a damp wicket but Henry Harrison, abetted by Warwickshire's lack of a specialist spinner, ground out a half-century to lift Surrey to 322. Jeeves "maintained a great pace throughout despite the trying conditions" according to the *Post* and finished with 24-9-70-4.

At the close, Warwickshire were 74/2 in their second innings with Quaife and Kinneir not out. If Surrey were to push for victory on the last day, they had to briskly dismiss two men who hated being dismissed.

Saturday brought the biggest crowd of the match and the occupants of the cheap seats were soon in full barracking mode. The overnight pair left, blocked and dabbed through the morning and well into the afternoon in a stand of 235. Kinneir scored an unbeaten 152 (two fives, 15 fours) and Quaife 109 (one five, eight fours – his second excruciating century of the match).

"Quaife became anxious in the eighties," reported the *Post*. "He occupied two hours in reaching his 50 and it was principally in singles that his score mounted to three figures from that point."

Warwickshire's declaration at 302/3 set Surrey an impossible target of 306 in 165 minutes. The game fizzled out into a draw but Jeeves, who dismissed Hayes for the second time in the match, had impressed the influential London press. Former Essex batsman Edward Sewell observed in *Cricket – A Weekly Record* that "Jeeves will get a sheaf of wickets by his quickness off the pitch: but he is not built for the Tom Richardson job". Sewell was referring to Jeeves's slight frame compared to Surrey stalwart Richardson, but he underestimated the all-rounder's wiry physique.

After bowling 47 overs in Southampton and 35 at The Oval, Jeeves delivered another 50 in the next game, a five-wicket defeat to Northamptonshire at Edgbaston. He carried the attack after Field was injured and Foster did not bowl due to the "effects of a strain" (he had been larking about at home with brother Arthur and collided with a sideboard). Colin Langley came into the team and "the Leamington amateur sent down an assortment of good, bad and indifferent balls that perplexed the batsmen considerably" but, with no spinner to tie up an end, Jeeves was lumbered with the stock-bowling role. His 50 overs cost only 101 runs, though just one wicket taken suggests his potency was blunted.

The burden remained squarely on Jeeves when Hampshire arrived at Edgbaston. Foster was "taking a much-needed holiday in North Wales" while Field lasted one session before falling ill. On an excellent batting wicket, Jeeves responded by dismissing five of Hampshire's top six. His 5-80 was "a capital performance under the circumstances", said the *Post* and, after Warwickshire replied to Hampshire's 246 with 187, Jeeves and Langley reduced the visitors to 52/7. Jeeves took three big wickets, removing openers Stone and Bowell and captain Edward

Sprot and took a wonderful catch to oust Robert Bolton (later chief constable of Northamptonshire). Warwickshire's six-wicket win owed much to Jeeves's match haul of 39-8-119-8.

Next day, against Sussex at Binley Road, Coventry, Jeeves enjoyed some respite. He was in the pavilion for much of the day as a 3,000 crowd watched Warwickshire amass 400. On the second morning Robert Relf kept Sussex afloat before he paid for underestimating Warwickshire's rising star. On 97, Relf took a single off the first ball of an over, exposing last man George Street to Jeeves. The next ball hit middle stump to leave the bowler with 30.2-12-72-4.

"The burden of the attack fell on Jeeves," reported the *Post*, "and it says much for the vitality of this young player that he developed a pace unusual for even him and was so fast that none but Relf could play him."

After Warwickshire were all out for 346 (Jeeves contributed a perky 29), at half past one on the final day, Sussex set off in pursuit of 480. Jeeves unleashed a ferocious new-ball spell. Philip Cartwright edged to Smith to leave Sussex 4/1 and, at the same score, Bert Wilson was dropped behind the wicket from successive balls. The fumbles were costly. Wilson survived to take the shine off the new ball before Joe Vine and Albert Relf added 152 to make the game safe. Sussex were 299/6 when the teams shook hands with the contest stone dead – though some members of the Coventry audience still felt cheated.

The *Post* reported that "at five minutes past six both captains agreed to close the game, a decision welcome to all the players and to the majority of the 5,000 spectators but resented by some".

Percy Jeeves had bowled 219.2 overs in five matches. With Frank Foster and Frank Field struggling, he was carrying a heavy workload in a gruelling schedule, but the treadmill was only just getting going. Next came successive away games against Middlesex, Kent and Yorkshire. That daunting tour, against three of the 'Big Six', was to bring Warwickshire little pleasure and a portion of humiliation. Few of their players emerged with credit. Jeeves did.

16.

A Turkish bath – Gaily decorated tents – Jeeves too good for Woolley – 16 all out

IT CAN never be known whether Percy Jeeves ever dreamed of playing at Lord's while he was regularly running through opponents' batting on behalf of Goole and Hawes. If he did, then on 16 June 1913, that dream came true. But it arrived accompanied by a lot of hard leather-chasing. Jeeves once suffered long and hard in the sun as a fielder with Goole as village batsmen made hay at Beverley. Now a similar experience fell his way against some of England's finest at the home of cricket.

Frank Foster returned to Warwickshire's team to face Middlesex (the captain's recovery aided, perhaps, by the prospect of a game at Lord's – slightly more alluring than Binley Road) and led them through a gruelling opening day in the field. Four thousand spectators sweltered in the open stands and the Bears' fielders baked in front of them as Middlesex plundered a perfect batting wicket. Openers William Robertson and Frank Tarrant rode their luck to add 178, Robertson scoring rapidly although, according to the *Post*, "the dangerous fast ball that Jeeves sends down in every over bothered him a lot and he was lucky on several occasions to snick it through the slips".

Robertson's luck ran out on 96 when Jeeves bowled him but Plum Warner and Patsy Hendren laid into a tiring attack to add 150 in 105 minutes. Warwickshire stuck at their work – "Foster, Hands and Jeeves maintained throughout a high standard of excellence" – but it became nothing more than a damage-limitation exercise when Billy Quaife came on to bowl his spin with a seven-man leg-side field. For the last half-hour, Jeeves was one of four fielders on the Grand Stand boundary as Quaife bowled for catches. Middlesex closed the day on 431/6.

On Tuesday morning they advanced to 483, an imposing total in the face of which Warwickshire struggled against cousins J.T. and J.W. (Jack and 'Young Jack') Hearne. It was 191/6 when Jeeves strode through the Long Room, down the pavilion steps and out to join Foster in the middle. With those two players, only one approach would do. They counter-attacked to add 82 in 65 minutes and, after Foster was bowled by Young Jack for 70, "the mantle fell upon Jeeves who was even more daring than his captain", reported the *Post*.

"He made the bowling look rather cheap and repeatedly got the ball close to the boundaries. On one occasion he failed by only a yard or so to place the ball over the rails on the uncovered stand side, no mean feat on a ground like Lord's." Jeeves scored 43 before lifting a catch to Rupert Anson, grandson of the Earl of Leicester.

After following on, 154 behind, Warwickshire closed the second day on 0/1. They required a huge rearguard action on the final day and needed everyone to contribute. First and foremost, they needed everyone there, but at start of play there was no sign of the captain.

Foster was no stranger to late nights or late arrivals (in a championship match at Harrogate in 1911 he took the field in the throes of a desperate hangover only after Frank Field threw him in a cold bath and gave him a rub-down). This latest tardiness was explained 97 years later in Robert Brooke's biography of Foster, *The Fields Were Sudden Bare*.

"Under the weather (again) after a heavy night, he had taken Willie Hands to the Turkish Baths early in the morning," wrote Brooke. "Then they treated themselves to a shave, haircut and shampoo, and had a game of snooker before deciding to get a cab to Lord's."

While that cab made its way through the London streets, 46-year-old Jack Hearne and young medium-pacer Guy Napier were making short work of Warwickshire's batting. Without a run added overnight, Crowther Charlesworth fell to Napier. Quaife, a potential match-saver, then fell for nine and from 16/3 Warwickshire plummeted to 17/7. Among the casualties was Jeeves, lbw to Hearne for one. At 20/8, Foster was still not ready to bat but while Santall and Hands eked 13 runs from the ninth wicket, the skipper at last got round to padding up. He went in at 33/9 and slogged 27 before Tarrant bowled Hands to leave Warwickshire all out for 63 on a perfect batting wicket. They were beaten by an innings and 91 runs and deeply embarrassed.

Alexandra Street Board School, Goole, where Jeeves underlined his talent with 33 wickets at 2.2 runs each.

Whitgift Church, past which 19-year-old Percy Jeeves and his team-mates sped on the way to a match on June 8, 1907. A clock was later added to the church in memory of men killed during the First World War.

The beautiful ground at Hawes Cricket Club, Wensleydale, where Percy Jeeves shone as a young player.

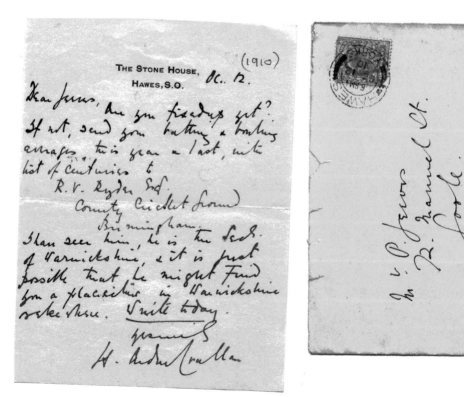

A letter from Hugh Arden Crallan urging Percy Jeeves to contact Warwickshire CCC.

Percy Jeeves's reference from Hugh Arden Crallan, roughed out by the landowner on Stone House notepaper.

That reference copied out in his best handwriting by Jeeves himself from his home address in Goole.

Percy Jeeves poses in his batting stance.

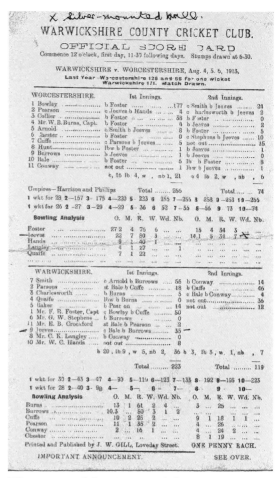

The scorecard from Warwickshire v Worcestershire in 1913 when Percy Jeeves's bowling earned him a silver-mounted ball.

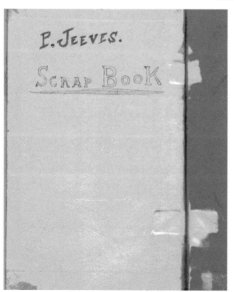

Percy Jeeves's scrapbook, now owned by author and collector David Frith to whom it was sent by Percy's younger brother Harold.

A signed photograph of Percy Jeeves.

Percy Jeeves showing the dapper style which caught the eye of writer PG Wodehouse at Cheltenham in 1913.

The 1913 and 1914 Wisdens owned and labelled by Percy Jeeves.

The Birmingham Pals, Percy Jeeves among them, gather beside Powell's Pool in Sutton Park, Birmingham, on October 30, 1914, at the start of their military training.

Platoon 9, C Company, the 15th Battalion, Royal Warwickshire Regiment. Percy Jeeves is seated third from the right on the front row.

The rough heathland of Sutton Park, this section near Powell's Pool where Percy Jeeves was based, was ideal for the training of men destined for the trenches.

<u>1916</u>

<u>July</u>

22nd   Battn. in Support as above.
   night of 22/23rd. Orders received from
          B'de re attack on east of HIGH WOOD.
          15th R. War.Regt. form details of
          B'de Reserve.
9.30   Battn. took up position in old German
p.m.   trench S.16 a-b and later, launched
          into front line to reinforce 1/R.West Kents
          & 14th R.War.Regt. "D" Coy formed part
          of the actual attack, going over the top,
          but lost heavily owing to Machine Gun
          fire from HIGH WOOD, & returned to
          original position. Capt. C.A.BILL &
          Capt.R.I.GOUGH were both wounded.
          Casualties 22/23rd Killed Off.1. O.Rs.
          13. Wounded Offrs.5. O.Rs.90.
          Missing Offr.1. O.Rs.31. Weather bright.

The entry in the battalion diary of the 15th Battalion, Royal Warwickshire Regiment, recording the raid in which Percy Jeeves lost his life.

Percy Jeeves pictured in the Goole Roll of Honour of men killed during the war.

The Thiepval Memorial to men killed on the Somme and whose remains were never found. It stands a short distance from where Percy Jeeves disappeared without trace.

The name of Percy Jeeves among those of his fellow fallen at the Thiepval Memorial.

The collapse was inexplicable. Foster's shoddiness was no excuse for the rest and there was some speculation that, all along, one or two players had an eye on Ascot races that afternoon. The *Post* was scathing: "Warwickshire had no excuse except a species of fright to advance for their sorry show." But around the corner lurked a performance which made a total of 63 appear positively imposing.

Next morning, over the county border at the elegant Angel Ground, Tonbridge, Warwickshire faced Kent for the first time in 14 years. The counties had fallen out in August 1899 during a grumpy affair at Catford Bridge in which Warwickshire's ten-wicket defeat featured a five-hour century by Quaife and, for the home side, 24 from Gerry Weigall, later to fail to spot Jeeves's talent in Harrogate.

The reason for ill feeling from that match is undocumented but the feud was stirred up again in 1911 when Warwickshire won the championship under a bizarre points system (proposed by Somerset) which meant that Kent finished only second despite winning most matches. Warwickshire took the title courtesy of a higher percentage of possible points gained.

Two years later, Kent were eager for revenge and bang in form. Top of the table, fresh from beating Essex the previous day and having won seven of their last eight games, they were full of confidence, as any side boasting Frank Woolley and Colin Blythe, great all-rounder and left-arm spinner respectively, had every right to be.

While Kent were at full strength, Warwickshire were badly weakened. Already without Kinneir, Hands, Field and Langley, they lost Smith with heatstroke from Lord's. That at least meant Jeeves had another pal alongside him on the trip as Len Bates came into the team. Jeeves had become close to Len, as he was to George Austin, now the regular scorer. He was becoming closer still to George's sister Annie.

After the imposing grandeur of Lord's, Tonbridge offered different but also considerable charm. The *Post* described "the pretty Angel ground with its crescent of gaily decorated tents and throng of motor cars before a crowd of nearly 4,000 people among whom the brilliant colours worn by the large number of ladies present imparted additional brightness to an already attractive scene". Kent's supporters expected a big win but Warwickshire fought hard on the opening day. On a poor wicket they made a competitive 262, Charlie Baker top-scoring with 59 while Jeeves's 30 included a straight six off fast bowler Arthur Day.

When Kent replied after tea, Jeeves was in the thick of the action. His third ball had 'Punter' Humphreys caught behind and he then caught Wally Hardinge off Foster in the slips. But it was with the very last ball of the day that he silenced the genteel audience. As Jeeves began his short, rhythmic run-up for the final time in the day, Kent's members were expecting to spend the evening happily anticipating Tonbridge-born Woolley making merry in the morning. But they were in for a shock as their hero was "caught in the slips off Jeeves's deadly fast ball".

One of 779 occasions on which Woolley was out caught in first-class cricket, the wicket left Kent uneasily placed at 40/3 at stumps. Straight from the Lord's debacle, Warwickshire had shown plenty of pluck.

On the second day rain permitted play for only an hour – long enough for Jeeves to come within a whisker of a most bizarre hat-trick. After a delayed start, his first ball of the day had James Seymour caught at slip, at which point lunch was taken. His previous delivery having dismissed Woolley the night before, the bowler was now on a very elongated hat-trick. Forty-five minutes later, Kent captain Ted Dillon faced the vital delivery – and defended it solidly. Kent progressed to 104/4 when the rain returned to wash out play.

With the match still not halfway through its second innings, for a decisive result to follow on Saturday, something extraordinary had to happen. It did. The sun came out and, as the *Post* correspondent put it, "6,000 people saw a termination to the Kent and Warwickshire fixture which must be classed among the most extraordinary ever recorded in first-class cricket".

On a drying pitch, Kent's last six first-innings wickets tumbled in 45 minutes as Foster took 5-13 in eight overs. All out for 132, the championship leaders trailed by 130 and were surprisingly on the back foot but the consensus in the press tent was that, against Blythe and Woolley on a treacherous track, Warwickshire would struggle to get 100, perhaps even 50, second time round. The consensus was right. They were all out for 16.

They began batting at noon and progressed smoothly to five without loss before Jack Parsons was stumped by Fred Huish off Woolley. Parsons's five was to remain the top score as Woolley and Blythe were simply unplayable. Jeeves went in at 12/4 and fell first ball, caught Blythe bowled Woolley: 12/5. Foster and Gerald Curle departed to successive balls from Blythe: 12/7. Hands was bowled by Woolley: 12/8. A buzz of excitement, the sort that only rises when something historic is unfolding, filled the Angel ground. Was Northamptonshire's record low total of 12 all out to be equalled?

Santall averted that prospect by edging a single but the end soon came. Warwickshire posted their smallest ever total and Woolley (5-1-8-5) and Blythe (5.2-1-8-5), having bowled the Bears out in 45 minutes, were cheered from the field.

Sixteen all out, the innings lasting just 62 balls, was risible but 147 appeared a difficult target on a pitch which had played all sorts of tricks on the batsmen. Jeeves soon took a stunning reflex catch at short leg off Foster to oust James Seymour and, at lunch, Kent were 16/2. The game was right in the balance.

During the interval, however, the wicket dried out and, with no specialist spinner to torment them, Kent galloped home. Woolley and Hardinge thrashed 57 in 25 minutes and the former advanced to a magnificent unbeaten 76. Only Jeeves came close to dismissing the great man. On 63, Woolley was "almost bowled by Jeeves and, off the next ball, Curle made a splendid attempt for a one-handed catch", but he survived to see his team to a remarkable win. Victory was sealed at 3.40pm with successive boundaries off Hands, at which point, reported the *Post*, "the crowd surged round the pavilion at close of play and would not be satisfied until their hero had bowed his acknowledgement".

While Woolley took the acclaim, Warwickshire's players packed quietly and quickly in the tiny away dressing rooms. A long train journey lay ahead and, all out for 62 and 16 in successive second innings, they had much to ponder as they travelled up to Sheffield to face mighty Yorkshire.

17.

The raucous regulars at Bramall Lane – "Some inspiring cricket was seen" – Jeeves hits Rhodes for successive sixes – A hero's reception

HAD GERRY Weigall been a better judge, the name Percy Jeeves would have been alongside those of George Hirst and Wilfred Rhodes on the home side of the scorecard when Yorkshire faced Warwickshire at Bramall Lane. Instead, Jeeves was among a visiting team which arrived in the Steel City to be perceived as cannon fodder by a partisan home crowd. Yorkshire's supporters, having read about the debacle in Tonbridge, anticipated a big win for their team. Warwickshire's batting was fragile and their bowling badly depleted. Already without the injured Frank Field and Colin Langley, the Bears now lost Willie Hands who was obliged to return to Birmingham on business.

After two miserable away defeats and a long train journey, Warwickshire could expect the going to be tough again in Sheffield – on and off the field. All Yorkshire crowds were raucous but at Bramall Lane, also home to Sheffield United Football Club, the regulars were the most scathing of all towards visitors. Nothing, though, could detract from Jeeves's excitement as he prepared to play senior cricket in the county of his birth for the first time.

On a humid morning, more than 5,000 people saw an eventful opening session which Yorkshire ended on 150/3. Jeeves took some early punishment from Roy Kilner who hit him for three fours in an over, albeit two sliced streakily through the slips. But Warwickshire hit back after lunch when Jeeves and Foster took the last five wickets for 24. Jeeves's third wicket, his 50th of the season, was unique. Percy Holmes, a 25-year-old batsman from Huddersfield in the first season of a career that was to bring 30,573 first-class runs, became the first and last batsman to be stumped off Jeeves in serious cricket.

Jeeves finished with 3-88 but failed with the bat when his team replied to Yorkshire's 274. Warwickshire reached 106/4 before William Booth, a bowler who shared Jeeves's ability to generate pace off the pitch, dismissed Charlie Baker and Eric Crockford with successive balls. Jeeves survived a loud appeal for caught-behind off the hat-trick ball but the reprieve was momentary. He was bowled by the next and, at the close, Warwickshire were 138/7.

Seventeen wickets on the first day were followed by 21 on the second but, among the floundering batsmen, Jeeves showed his native county what they were missing. He batted with a verve which delighted even Yorkshire's supporters and threatened to transform the match until he was undone by his own naivety.

First, he impressed with the ball. Yorkshire's second innings stumbled to 7/2 as Jeeves, "bowling at a great pace", hit the leg stumps of Ben Wilson and David Denton with the third and sixth balls of his first over. Kilner blasted 74 in 50 minutes before he was bowled by Jeeves, who also castled Holmes to finish with four wickets for 76. "Though Foster and Jeeves had to accept punishment," reported the *Yorkshire Post*, "they both sent down a good many difficult balls."

Warwickshire required 298 to win, a difficult target on a worn wicket in light which was poor to start with and became murkier still. The chase stumbled to 86/6 before Jeeves joined Crockford at the crease and, according to the *Birmingham Daily Post*, "some inspiring cricket was seen, which did much to redeem Warwickshire's damaged reputation".

Yorkshire reject Jeeves took with relish to the bowling of Warwickshire reject Rhodes. Left-arm spinner Rhodes had become one of English cricket's dominant figures since the Bears' committee declined to offer him a contract following a trial in 1897. He was admired throughout England and idolised in Yorkshire but now suffered the indignity of seeing the ball twice disappear back over his head into the crowd. "Jeeves was in his most aggressive mood," reported the *Birmingham Daily Post*, "and not long after his arrival, startled the crowd by hitting two successive sixes off Rhodes into the football grand stand. He followed this feat with several other fine boundary hits."

Even the notoriously abrasive Sheffield audience relished the resistance. "Jeeves's two straight drives for six off Rhodes made him quite a hero in the eyes of the Bramall Lane crowd," the paper added. "He appeared to revel in displaying his prowess at the expense of his native county."

As his partnership grew with the steady Crockford, Warwickshire's total passed 150 for the loss of six wickets. An unlikely victory began to loom into sight but the ball was becoming increasingly difficult to see. In 1924, Warwickshire and England wicketkeeper Dick Lilley wrote in his reminiscences *24 Years of Cricket*, that the light was often poor at Bramall Lane due to the "nature and proximity of the local manufactories".

Add in thick cloud and now it was almost dark but neither of the young batsmen thought to appeal against the light which, under the regulations of the day, the onus was on them to do. As umpires Dick Barlow and Henry Bagshaw allowed play to go on, Jeeves continued to connect with remarkable clarity in the gloom until, on 42, he cover-drove Booth and fell to a stunning, one-handed catch by Rhodes. Jeeves received a hero's reception back into the pavilion.

Crockford was soon bowled by a Drake delivery that he simply didn't see and stumps were drawn, with Warwickshire 176/8, to frustrated cries of "play it out" from the crowd. The home side took just 40 minutes to complete an 89-run victory next morning but, as Yorkshire's supporters settled into the pubs to dissect the match on Saturday lunchtime, among all the triumphalism was talk of one that had got away.

18.

Tedious batting from Makepeace – The suffering of Hastings Post Office – "Is Jeeves over-bowled?" – A broken stump

WARWICKSHIRE HAD shown greater resolve in Sheffield than in their capitulations in the south but three defeats, including humiliation at Tonbridge, sent them towards back-to-back home games under pressure. Concerns were growing that too many of the team of recent champions were over the hill. Foster's side had much to prove in the home double-header against Lancashire at Edgbaston and Gloucestershire at Nuneaton. They won both matches but thanks not to a stirring of the old guard but 16 wickets from Percy Jeeves.

In his first full season, Jeeves was, to say the least, earning his corn. Having already delivered 384.2 overs, comfortably more than any other Warwickshire bowler, he ploughed through another 53.1 (very effectively too, taking 4-64 and 4-55) against Lancashire. His accuracy rendered the powerful Red Rose batting line-up strokeless. On the second day, according to the *Post*, "the cricket simply dragged tediously along until a successful objection to the very bad light caused a welcome break at quarter past five".

Everton and England footballer Harry Makepeace was the main culprit as he crawled to 46 in 130 minutes. "The international footballer was timorous to an extraordinary degree," lamented the paper. "It cannot truthfully be said that his dismissal, at 136, after surviving more than one confident lbw appeal, was received with regret."

Warwickshire won by two wickets and kept up the momentum at Nuneaton next day. In only the second championship match to be played at Nuneaton Cricket Club, Jeeves and Foster were presented with a deadly slow wicket upon which to bowl. But they somehow prised enough life from it to share the ten Gloucestershire wickets.

The crowd, including many miners and swollen by interest created by the inclusion of local fast bowler Tom Hilditch, were a boisterous bunch and roared their support for the Bears' attack. At first, they had little to cheer as openers Charles Barnett and Alf Dipper added 113 but then Jeeves held a screamer at second slip off Foster to dismiss Barnett. One run later, Dipper edged Foster and again Jeeves clung on. After Michael Green's leg stump was uprooted by Jeeves, the visitors went into lunch at 133/3. Gloucestershire were wobbling and, in the first hour of the afternoon session, they were rolled over. With the crowd baying, Jeeves was rampant.

In his second over he bowled Tom Miller and had Tom Langdon caught at point. That brought in John Nason, a destructive hitter as Hastings Post Office discovered in 1908 when he opened for University School against them and clobbered 97 of the first 99 runs. This time he hurried to 34 but was then bowled "attempting a wretched stroke" by Jeeves. The all-rounder added the wickets of Tommy Gange and Charlie Parker in successive overs to end with 26.2-6-94-6 as Gloucestershire were bowled out for 249. Only a bowler of the highest class could have summoned such devil from a lifeless track.

After Jack Parsons's maiden century helped build a first-innings lead of 98, the Bears went on to close out victory by eight wickets. Jeeves added another two wickets on the final day when Hilditch, to great local joy, took 3-41, figures which were to remain the best of a Warwickshire career which spanned only eight matches.

Foster's team had bounced back impressively in the two home matches but next up at Edgbaston were Kent and even a first-day wash-out could not save Warwickshire from another drubbing by a team heading for its third title in five years.

The Bears again succumbed to the destroyers of Tonbridge. Blythe harvested 32-13-47-5 and Woolley 30.3-8-75-5 as Warwickshire mustered only 159. As Kent replied with 371/8, the heavy workload upon Jeeves started to take its toll. On his way to 27.2-4-90-3, the *Post* reported, he "stuck to his work for an hour without a break and bowled until he was tired out".

At least he was permitted a slightly longer rest at lunch on the second day when the interval was expanded by 15 minutes to mark the death of the Right Honourable Alfred Lyttelton. A former MCC president and MP for Warwick and Leamington, Lyttelton was a devout cricket-lover, whose family home was at nearby Hagley. To commemorate his passing, the pavilion flag was lowered to half-mast. It might have been for Warwickshire's batting. All out for 161 second time round, they were beaten by an innings and 51 runs.

A couple of days off was all Jeeves needed to regain his zest, as Leicestershire batsman Bill Shipman discovered to his cost when Warwickshire visited Hinckley. Leicestershire piled up 392 but Jeeves took 5-109, his second victim, Shipman, falling to a delivery "of great pace, removing the middle stump and sending a bail a measured distance of 38 paces away".

At the close of Saturday's opening day's play, Warwickshire were nine without loss in reply to a large total which would have been immense without the toil of Jeeves. Back in Birmingham, the evening *Sports Argus* posed a pertinent question: "IS JEEVES OVER-BOWLED?"

The emergence of this potent young addition to the attack had certainly been timely. Field and Santall were ageing, Foster unpredictable and Hands and Langley often unavailable due to business, so the arrival of a high-quality bowler of unlimited willingness was the answer to Warwickshire's prayers. But he needed sensible handling, argued 'Argus Junior'.

"With F.R. Foster off his form, Field off ill and W.C. Hands and C.K. Langley available for very few matches, Warwickshire are truly suffering considerable handicaps from the bowling point of view. But there promises to be a further disaster. Young Jeeves is being overworked and nothing will kill a young bowler so easily as overwork. He is young and enthusiastic and would not think of complaining, I feel sure, but it should not be for him to have to complain. A fast bowler always wants careful nursing, especially when he is young, and that is not what Jeeves is getting. Already this season he has bowled more than 500 overs and, more often than not, has been kept on for such long spells at the start of a match that afterwards he has been stiff and 'off it'. That is not fair and however weak the remaining resources of the side, he should have his fair share of rest. I feel confident that were he put on for six overs and rested for six overs alternately he would be more successful than he is under the present high pressure. He might not take more wickets but he would not be scored from so freely."

Jeeves was certainly not over-bowled two days later when Warwickshire lost 20 wickets in less than five hours on Monday to lose to Leicestershire by an innings and 21 runs. It was another pitiful batting display, though Jeeves emerged with credit. In the first innings he scored 21. In the second he shared in a stand of 95 in 45 minutes with Charlesworth.

"Jeeves was credited with the most virile display of the match," said the *Post*. "He had been one of few to accomplish anything of value in the first innings and when he went in again he was in very militant mood." On his way to his maiden half-century, exactly 50, he hit nine fours and twice lifted left-armer William Brown for six.

Foster evidently read the *Sports Argus*. In Warwickshire's next game, against Derbyshire at Edgbaston, the captain and Field bowled unchanged to dismiss the visitors for 95. The respite did Jeeves no harm at all. In the second innings he delivered 12-4-21-1 and the wicket he took was spectacular. Derbyshire captain Tom Forrester (educated in Small Heath and who played 26 matches for the Bears as an amateur in the late 1890s) was bowled by a ball so rapid that it broke a stump in two.

Warwickshire completed an innings-and-31-runs victory over Derbyshire on 22 July 1913. Halfway through his first season as a county cricketer, Percy Jeeves had plenty upon which to reflect with pride and much to look forward to with excitement. He had taken effortlessly to first-class cricket and was already being spoken of as the likely sixth Warwickshire player to be selected for England. Within three years, surely, he would follow Dick Lilley, Billy Quaife, Frank Foster, Tiger Smith and Septimus Kinneir to the honour of representing England on a cricket field.

But exactly three years later, on 22 July 1916, Percy Jeeves would be in a different field, a cornfield, in France, with shells and bullets filling the air around him in the final moments of his life.

19.

485 runs and 19 wickets in a day – "Deadly bowling by Jeeves" – Yorkshire's players speak highly of Jeeves's batting – To Cheltenham

THE BALL which shattered Tom Forrester's leg stump supplied Percy Jeeves with his 70th wicket of 1913. Already past the cherished 100-wicket milestone for the season were Colin Blythe (Kent), George Thompson (Northamptonshire), Albert Relf (Sussex), Frank Tarrant (Middlesex), Harry Dean (Lancashire), William Booth (Yorkshire) and John Hitch (Surrey), all experienced, high-class players. Could Jeeves, in his first season, join this illustrious list?

He moved significantly closer in the next match, against Lancashire at Old Trafford. He took 5-84 in the first innings before "making the ball fly about a great deal" in the second, striking the lugubrious Harry Makepeace numerous blows on the body.

Jeeves also recorded his second first-class half-century. Warwickshire's second innings was meandering along at 219/7, 74 ahead of the Red Rose, when Jeeves joined Eric Crockford at the crease. Just as they had done at Sheffield, the pair counter-attacked vigorously. Against tiring bowlers, under the rarity of a searing Manchester sun, the eighth-wicket partnership added 85 in 65 minutes. Jeeves lifted Makepeace for six before falling to a catch by young Harry Edge (playing the first of his only three first-class matches), right on the rope, for 53.

With a five-for and a half-century in the match, far from looking tired, Jeeves was warming up nicely for back-to-back home games much-anticipated by both the county club and him personally. Next up at Edgbaston were local rivals Worcestershire, the team against which he made his championship debut. Then it was Yorkshire, Jeeves's native county and a big draw in Birmingham for several reasons.

Warwickshire's supporters were always attracted by the charismatic White Rose with so many famous players, but the fixture had extra spice. The Bears fans were still keen to see their players repay some of the misery meted out to them in bizarre fashion in May 1896 when Yorkshire amassed 887 at Edgbaston. Lord Hawke killed the match stone dead by allowing his team to bat throughout the first two days, a curious strategy by a man famous for his win-at-all-costs mentality and one which still rankled in the Edgbaston stands.

First came Worcestershire and the opening day attracted more than 10,000 spectators who were rewarded with some thrilling cricket: 485 runs and 19 wickets. By lunchtime, the visitors, put in, had already galloped to 200/3 with Fred Bowley having hit the bowling to all parts for 136. Then their last seven wickets fell in an hour to Foster and Jeeves. Bowley made 177 with 27 fours, five threes and 14 twos then became one of Foster's six victims while, according to the *Post*: "Jeeves did not bowl as well as usual but claimed three wickets and made a very smart right-handed catch low down in the slips which dismissed Pearson."

After Worcestershire were all out for 266, Warwickshire dipped to 133/7 before the same two players bailed them out again. Foster hit 50 and Jeeves was 33 not out overnight having "hit with his customary vigour and sent up the 200 with a straight drive for six over the pavilion rails off Cuffe".

An astonishing opening day ended: Worcestershire 266, Warwickshire 219/9. Day two brought more spectacular cricket; a Warwickshire victory which prompted the headline: "DEADLY BOWLING BY JEEVES". The Yorkshireman took a career-best 7-34 as Worcestershire were skittled for 74.

They reached 26/0, at which point Jeeves had 0-16. Thereafter he was "practically unplayable". He induced a fatal edge from Bowley, had Fred Pearson caught in the slips, bowled captain William Burns and deceived Frank Chester into sending up a skier to third man. Successive yorkers hit the stumps of Fred Hunt and Richard Burrows and another, with the hat-trick ball, saw a huge lbw shout against Ernie Bale turned down. Bale fell to Foster but Jeeves trapped rabbit Arthur Conway lbw to finish with 14.1-5-34-7.

It was bowling of high pace but also high skill. "In the first innings the Yorkshireman was rather below his usual standard," reported the *Post*, "but when Worcestershire went in a second time Jeeves had recovered his form. He stuck to no standard pattern in his attack. Throughout the innings he used his brains and varied the pace and direction of almost every delivery and never gave the batsmen a moment's ease."

Jeeves's magnificent work set up a seven-wicket win and earned him a silver-mounted ball which resides in the museum at Edgbaston to this day. It also sent him full of confidence into the Yorkshire game and, two days after registering his best bowling figures in first-class cricket, Jeeves recorded his highest score.

At Bramall Lane, earlier in the season, he had shown Yorkshire a glimpse of his batting prowess. Further evidence followed when they arrived at Edgbaston.

The White Rose county fielded an unexpected addition to their bowling attack, 34-year-old Rockley Wilson, a master at Winchester School, recalled for the first time in 11 years. On the opening day, his whimsical spin brought six wickets to reduce Warwickshire to 190/7. Jack Parsons, Crowther Charlesworth and Charlie Baker holed out to donkey-drops and when Wilson dismissed George Stephens and Eric Crockford for ducks, the Bears were in deep trouble as Jeeves went in to join Billy Quaife.

As Quaife batted with his customary caution, Jeeves also deployed some restraint. His batting was usually belligerent, bordering on gung-ho, but this time his aggression was selective. The result – an unbeaten 86 made in 105 minutes without a false stroke. He drove Wilson into the pavilion for six, hit 12 fours and a five and dealt alike with Wilson's eccentric twirl and the high-class fare of William Booth and Wilfred Rhodes with such aplomb that he looked set fair for a maiden century. Sadly, he ran out of partners but Jeeves had unveiled a new dimension to his cricket.

"His reputation as a batsman has principally been as a hitter, due perhaps to the fact that generally wickets have been falling rapidly when he has gone in," commented the *Post*. "But yesterday he appeared in a different light. Judgement was the outstanding feature of his batting and his display was by far the soundest he has yet given for Warwickshire. The northerners allowed the young professional to slip through their fingers. They failed to detect the latent ability of the youth and Warwickshire's gain was indeed Yorkshire's loss.

"The fact that Jeeves has already taken 91 wickets at a comparatively cheap rate in his first season establishes his claim to be regarded as a player of unusual promise. But in case the Yorkshire authorities had overlooked that fact, Jeeves took advantage of their visit to Edgbaston to demonstrate his ability."

The opposition was suitably impressed, as revealed by the correspondent of the *Yorkshire Post*.

"Yorkshire's players speak highly of Jeeves's batting," he wrote, "as indeed they are entitled to do for it was about the best individual effort they have had put up against them this year. I imagine that, after his performance, Jeeves will have a higher place than No.9 in the batting list. He certainly is a better bat than some of the men who habitually go in earlier."

Warwickshire's supporters loved the spectacle of this free-spirited young man laying into Yorkshire's swaggering bowlers. It was something of an anti-climax when heavy rain on Saturday saw the match peter out to a draw, but Jeeves had enjoyed a brilliant week. He was improving all the time and next came new terrain – a short journey to the Cotswolds to face Gloucestershire at Cheltenham. And there lay a twist of fortune which would immortalise the name of this modest young sportsman.

The residents of the spa town included the parents of writer Pelham Grenville Wodehouse – and 'Plum' was in England for a visit. The paths of Percy Jeeves and Pelham Grenville Wodehouse were about to cross, briefly and indirectly. As far as we know, they did not even speak, yet their fleeting acquaintance would leave an indelible imprint upon English literature and the English language.

20.

Asquith vetoes Channel Tunnel scheme – A sea of boaters – Gloucestershire crack open the champagne – P.G. Wodehouse takes note

B Y THE summer of 1913, P.G. Wodehouse was beginning to make his name in Britain and the United States as a writer of light comedy. He had published 17 books, mainly of school stories, spent some years contributing a humorous column to London's *Globe* evening newspaper and written lyrics for musical comedies.

For the first half of 1913, Wodehouse divided his time between England and New York where he had spent much of the previous two years trying to become established. He began the year in London but, after his first attempt to write for the West End – the play *Brother Alfred* at the Savoy Theatre – flopped, he returned to the States. He had made several trips to New York, trying to get his work known over there, and went over again on the SS *Olympic* on 30 April. He sold some short stories to magazines during the following month before travelling back to England in June.

Wodehouse spent the summer at his lodgings at 2 Queen's Club Terrace in Barons Court, West London – but on Thursday 14 August he awoke in Cheltenham. He was staying at his parents' house, 3 Wolseley Terrace, a white, three-storeyed property in a row five minutes from the centre of town.

He was not fond of Cheltenham and not close to his parents who had been thousands of miles away for much of his childhood. 'Plum' was brought up mainly by a succession of aunts and uncles while his father pursued a career as a civil servant in Hong Kong. The distance between Plum and his parents, especially his formidable mother, was never recovered. When they moved to Cheltenham in 1902, following his father's retirement, he was indifferent to the move and was to spend little time there. But there was one magnet capable of drawing him to the town – its cricket festival. Cricket was one of Wodehouse's deepest passions and no lover of the sport could resist the charm of the Cheltenham College Ground in festival week.

Gloucestershire were due to start a match against Warwickshire and the writer looked forward to the day's play as he perused the morning paper to see what his colleagues in journalism had unearthed. They reported that Prime Minister Herbert Asquith had vetoed French proposals to build a tunnel under the English Channel. Other headlines included: "Baby attacked by baboon"; "Chicago policewomen – disadvantage of skirts"; "Wife sold for ten shillings".

After breakfast, Wodehouse descended the steps from number three, strolled along narrow Wolseley Terrace, crossed over and turned into Oriel Street. He turned right into Bath Road, busy with carriages and motor cars heading towards the cricket ground. A stream of pedestrians flowed towards the college for the opening day of the third and last match of a festival which was heading for unprecedented success on and off the field.

The home team had an opportunity to make history. Never in the festival's 36-year history had Gloucestershire won all three games, but the achievement was within reach after victories over Worcestershire and Hampshire by 129 runs and 39 runs respectively. Those matches attracted large attendances. From six days' cricket so far, the festival had generated a greater profit than from all nine days together in 1912.

A successful team always attracted people but the bigger crowds were also due to changes to the organisation of the festival. For the first time, privileges were given to Gloucestershire members. They were allocated their own stand in front of the gymnasium on the college lawn, along with an enclosure with refreshments provided exclusively for them by George's the caterers.

Following a good response to letters sent to local businessmen inviting them to entertain clients at the festival, there were more private hospitality tents than ever before. A village of white marquees filled one end of the ground.

The rest was open to the public and, as the 12.15pm start of play approached, the stands were well-populated. On a sunny day there was hardly a bare head in sight with a sea of boaters and ladies' more lavish hats.

As Wodehouse settled into his seat, a short distance away, Percy Jeeves prepared in the away professionals' dressing room. As always, Warwickshire's team had split their rail-travel and accommodation arrangements. The amateurs travelled first class while the professionals went third. In Cheltenham, the amateurs – Frank Foster, Charles Baker, Eric Crockford and Willie Hands – were staying at the salubrious Belle Vue Hotel in High Street, while the professionals took humbler lodgings. Two of Gloucestershire's star players, Gilbert Jessop and Charles Barnett, unavailable for this game, had just checked out of the Belle Vue after the win over Hampshire.

The amateurs and professionals also changed separately at the ground and entered the field through different gates. For Jeeves, the affluent atmosphere of the College Ground was redolent of country house cricket at Hawes, but on a much grander scale.

After Gloucestershire captain Cyril Sewell won the toss, his team spent the first day moving quietly into command. For once, Jeeves went wicketless in his opening spell and, by lunch, 928 people had paid for admission and Alf Dipper was on his way to a colourless century. Dipper was assisted by poor fielding to which Jeeves was a notable exception, but the all-rounder enjoyed no success with the ball. Even when brought back late in the day, with Gloucestershire 263/8, he could not prevent the tail wagging. Jeeves took a fine catch, gallantly standing at short leg to the deadly slow spin of Quaife, to dismiss wicketkeeper Harry Smith for 56, but even then last pair Charlie Parker and George Dennett added 46 to lift Gloucestershire to 328.

Jeeves ended with 17-4-43-0, well and truly back down to earth after posting career-bests in the previous two matches. But on one of his least successful days in county cricket, he had made a vivid and lasting impression on one spectator.

Heavy rain in the early hours of Friday morning left the College Ground pitch treacherous and 22 wickets fell on the second day. Warwickshire resumed on 34/1. After 30 minutes of left-arm spin from Dennett and Parker they were 48/5. Jeeves went in, took a single off Dennett, then received an unplayable ball – pitched leg, hit off – from Parker; 49/6. Warwickshire were all out for 135 at 1.25pm but Sewell did not enforce the follow-on. Gloucestershire were keen to ensure there would be some cricket on Saturday when they expected "a big sixpenny gate".

By lunchtime on Friday, 929 people had paid for admission (the same 928 as on Thursday, perhaps, plus a friend) and early in the afternoon session, they saw a little success for Jeeves. Gloucestershire were 47/1 when he replaced Foster at the Chapel End and, in his second over, had Tom Langdon caught by the captain at second slip. Foster then led a fightback with six wickets but Jeeves was lightly used, finishing with 7-1-12-1. He took two exceptional slip-catches though and Sewell departed shaking his head in disbelief after falling to a brilliant take, low and right-handed, in poor light.

Gloucestershire were 172 all out at 5.15pm, after which the light deteriorated sharply, much to Warwickshire's cost. Chasing 367 to win, they were three down for 24 at the close after Dennett removed Tiger Smith, Jack Parsons and Crowther Charlesworth in the gloom.

On a cool, dull Saturday morning, Gloucestershire quickly completed their historic festival full house. Baker, who combined his career in cricket with one as a music hall artist and was soon to sing before the Cheltenham Footlights, was caught by wicketkeeper Robinson off Gange: 37/4. Foster and Quaife added 18 in ten minutes then the former slashed Gange high to substitute Jack Bowles at third man: 55/5. In went Jeeves – and edged his first ball to the wicket keeper. The church clock was striking one when Warwickshire's last wicket fell. They were all out for 119 and beaten by 247 runs to the sound of mighty cheering from the home supporters.

Gloucestershire were applauded from the field and the committee cracked open two bottles of champagne, generously extending the contents to the professionals as well as the amateurs in their team. A toast was drunk: "Success to Cheltenham and the County Club."

Percy Jeeves boarded the train back to Birmingham with a haul of one run and one wicket in the match. It was much the least productive of his 22 first-class games so far, yet his appearance at Cheltenham was to gain his name immortality. Three years later, P.G. Wodehouse conceived two new characters – a foppish aristocrat and his immaculate manservant – for a series of short stories. The former, he called Bertie Wooster. When considering a name for the latter, Wodehouse's mind emulated that of Sir Arthur Conan Doyle, who named 240 characters after professional cricketers. His thoughts strayed back to Cheltenham, 1913, and the impressive figure cut by one of the players at the College Ground.

More than half a century later, with Jeeves and Wooster established in the pantheon of the nation's literary favourites, Rowland Ryder, son of the Warwickshire secretary who had discovered Jeeves at Hawes, wrote to Wodehouse to ask whether he really did name the character after the cricketer. On 26 October 1967, from his home in Remsenburg, New York, Wodehouse dispatched a reply.

> "Dear Mr Ryder,
> Yes, you are quite right. It must have been in 1913 that I paid a visit to my parents in Cheltenham and went to see Warwickshire play Gloucestershire on the Cheltenham College ground. I suppose Jeeves's bowling must have impressed me, for I remembered him in 1916 when I was in New York and starting the Jeeves and Bertie saga, and it was just the name I wanted.
> I have always thought till lately that he was playing for Gloucestershire that day. (I remember admiring his action very much.)
> Yours sincerely,
> PG Wodehouse."

That letter is still in the possession of Warwickshire County Cricket Club and is on display in the museum at Edgbaston.

21.

A former bricklayer deploys tedious methods – Doll is the 100th – A downpour at twenty past two – Jeeves gets a pay rise

OBLIVIOUS TO the momentous seed sown, Percy Jeeves immediately turned his attention to another major challenge. Two days after their defeat at Cheltenham, Warwickshire faced Surrey at Edgbaston and again confronted cricket's most illustrious opening pair – Tom Hayward and Jack Hobbs. Six weeks earlier, Hayward had become only the second player, after W.G. Grace, to make 100 first-class hundreds. Hobbs was already viewed by many as capable of relieving W.G. of his mantle of the greatest ever batsman. The two Surrey kingpins were among England's finest batsmen – and Jeeves dismissed them both on his way to another five-for.

Such prestige opposition attracted another bumper crowd to Edgbaston and the opening-day spectators were not disappointed. Surrey batted first and Frank Foster and Frank Field were comfortably seen off before Jeeves quickly knocked Hayward out of his comfort zone. In his first over, he bowled him for 20. Hobbs was in sublime form, driving lusciously to race to 122 out of 199. In this mood, he appeared impossible to restrain, never mind dismiss, but Jeeves got one to deviate just a fraction, Hobbs drove and edged to third slip. A great batsman in great nick, defeated.

Almost single-handedly, Jeeves restricted Surrey to a modest total of 324 as he added the scalps of William Spring, Bert Strudwick and Bill Hitch. Strudwick, bowled for a duck, was the bowler's 100th wicket in first-class cricket. When Hitch sliced to slip, Jeeves was on 98 for the season after finishing with 22-5-60-5, excellent figures no doubt noted from afar by Mr Wodehouse as he studied the paper next day.

After centuries by Crowther Charlesworth and Billy Quaife lifted Warwickshire's reply to 312, the match drifted towards stalemate. Surrey's intentions were clear from the last 45 minutes of the second day when the scoreboard appeared to freeze. After Hobbs was run out for nine, Hayward and Ernie Hayes crawled to 19/1 from 15 overs by Foster and Jeeves.

On the final day the visitors killed the game stone dead to ensure they collected three points for having the first-innings lead in a draw. It was deadly dull stuff for the spectators with former bricklayer Henry Harrison the main culprit. Never an attractive batsman ("a very correct player – so correct that he played his shots mostly to the fielders", team-mate Andrew Sandham once quipped) he was loudly barracked by the 3,000-strong crowd as he met every ball, good and bad, with defence.

"In the first innings Harrison attracted attention to himself by his tedious methods," reported the *Post*, "but yesterday he eclipsed the achievements of everybody else by staying at the crease for three hours 55 minutes, making 79. In a similar period at Worcester, a short time ago, Braund made 257."

Jeeves ended the innings with 1-30 from 19 overs so went into Warwickshire's last home game of the summer, against Middlesex, still requiring one wicket for 100 in his first season. What a remarkable achievement that would be for a cricketer who, but for one strange quirk of fate, would still be mowing the grounds of The Stone House, Hawes and lamenting his fruitless trial at Harrogate.

The vital wicket eluded him on a one-sided opening day in which Warwickshire made 187 (Jeeves hit the younger Jack Hearne on to the roof of the covered stand in a breezy 17) before Middlesex replied with 156/1. Next day, the visitors strengthened their grip on the match and were in complete control at 311/5 when Mordaunt Doll, on seven, faced Jeeves.

An Old Carthusian and Cambridge blue, Doll had recently posted his maiden first-class century, against Nottinghamshire at Lord's. He was a clean hitter but suspect in defence and when he received a brisk sphere which darted in from outside off stump, his middle peg was sent flying. Jeeves had pouched his 100th wicket in the grand manner and the spectators rose to salute a player they had quickly taken to their hearts for his talent, courtesy and his endless capacity for honest toil.

Jeeves's milestone was the only highlight of an untidy performance by Warwickshire to end their home fixtures. They lost by an innings and 37 runs, their tenth defeat of the season, and defeat number 11 followed immediately against Sussex at Hove where the batting failed abjectly yet again.

The Bears were dismissed for 132 and, although Jeeves took three quick wickets on the first evening, Sussex recovered to reach 332. The Hove enclosure, flags flying, seagulls circling, deckchairs rippling, was a glorious sight in lovely late-summer sunshine and Warwickshire had some time to enjoy an extra stroll along the beach into Brighton after their six-wicket defeat was completed just after 3pm on the final day.

Jeeves's first season of championship cricket closed at Northampton. Two years earlier, that venue was the setting for Warwickshire's greatest day as they clinched their first title. A year later, Northamptonshire were the opposition for Jeeves's first appearance on a championship field, as a substitute fielder for six balls at Edgbaston. This time, Wantage Road offered little for the memory bank – just three days of rain and gloom.

In 200 minutes' play on the first day, with batting linchpin 'Fanny' Walden away with Tottenham Hotspur preparing for their Division One game against Sheffield United, Northamptonshire made a meagre 224. Jeeves added the wickets of Stuart Humphrey (later an eye specialist in Northampton) and Walter Buswell to his season's tally. On the second day, Warwickshire replied with 237, Jeeves driving handsomely for 34, before the home side opened their second innings with identical twins William and John Denton. The latter's off stump was dislodged by Jeeves who also took a catch at short leg to give his pal Len Bates his first county victim, Trinidadian left-hander Sydney Smith. Bates, an elegant batsman who hated bowling, was to add only eight more wickets in a career spanning 444 first-class matches.

Northamptonshire inched to 177/3 at the close of the second day – and that was that for the season. On the final day, there was no play before lunch which was taken at half past one. A terminal downpour at 2.20pm brought the season to a close.

Warwickshire had never threatened to regain the title they had won in such thrilling fashion only two years earlier. They dropped from ninth to 11th in the championship, losing 11 of 24 games, more than in the previous two seasons combined. They were highly erratic, yet crowds, attracted by the cavalier cricket of Foster and Jeeves, held up well. Membership topped 2,000 for the first time and a profit of over £600 was recorded.

In his first season in the team, Jeeves was one of only three ever-presents, alongside Charlesworth and Baker. He scored 765 runs at an average of 20.13 and took 106 wickets at 20.88 each. It was a debut season in which his cricket was invariably very good and laced with sporadic brilliance. The committee recognised his worth. When 12-month engagements were handed out for 1913/14, Percy Jeeves was awarded an annual salary of £85, the same as long-established team-mates Santall, Smith, Charlesworth and Baker. Of the professionals, only the veteran Quaife (£125) was paid more.

22.

An interview with Percy Jeeves

IT WAS a wonderful first summer for the modest son of a railwayman and Percy Jeeves returned to Goole with much to report to his proud family and friends. Maybe he even caught up with his first public critic – the *Goole Times*'s garrulous 'Spectator'.

For Percy's brothers who with him had long devoured sports magazines, November brought a special issue to enjoy. Warwickshire's veteran bowler and coach Sydney Santall dabbled in journalism and he seized the opportunity to interview his young team-mate for the magazine *Cricket – A Weekly Record*. The publication, priced 2d, bore a quotation from Byron, "Together joined in Cricket's manly toil", on its masthead and beneath that noble phrase, on the front page of the edition of Saturday 15 November 1913, was: "A Chat with Percy Jeeves".

Here, in its entirety, is Jeeves's only ever interview which includes a rather different and more prosaic version to that advanced by Rowland Ryder of how his move to Warwickshire came about.

"Few cricketers of late years have met with such remarkable success in their first season in first-class cricket as Percy Jeeves, the young Yorkshireman who has thrown in his lot with the Warwickshire County Club.

"Last season, Jeeves accomplished the great feat of capturing 106 wickets at 20.88 runs each and scoring 765 runs with an average of 20.13 per innings. He is a fast-medium right-hand bowler with an action which old cricketers say is very similar to that of 'Merry' Preston, the former Yorkshire bowler of 25 years ago. He has a nice run-up to the wicket, a very loose arm and a beautiful body swing and makes the ball go away very quickly with his arm. His batting is of the forcing type and, although not by any means a big man, he hits the ball tremendously hard. What has been Yorkshire's loss is Warwick's gain and good judges consider that, given good health, Jeeves may well gain the highest honours on the cricket field.

"When I looked up Jeeves for the purpose of this interview he had just returned from playing in a football match when his side had not only received a good trouncing, but a good drenching. After we had made some uncomplimentary remarks about the weather, for the rain was still coming down in sheets, I told him the nature of my mission and he was willing enough to talk, as I was not exactly a stranger.

"In appearance, Jeeves has nothing of the typical sturdy Yorkshireman about him. He has clean-cut features and, standing about 5 feet 8 inches, only weighs just over ten and a half stone but he is well-knit and athletic in build.

'Where and when were you born?'

'Earlsheaton, near Dewsbury, on March 5, 1888.'

'Do you come from a cricketing family?'

'No, my father never played and my two brothers only occasionally.'

'For what teams did you play in your boyhood?'

'I can remember very little of my cricket at Earlsheaton but when my father moved to Goole in 1901 I became a member of the Alexandra Street School's team and for them I was fairly successful. In 1902 I was asked to play for the 2nd XI of the town club and got six wickets for 25 runs in my first match. I was only 14 at the time. When the next season came round I had left school and immediately got a place in the Goole first eleven.'

'What was your best performance with the Goole club?'

'It's so long ago I hardly remember but I believe my best score was 63 against Swanland Manor.'

'You were more of a bat than a bowler in those days then?'

'Oh yes. Though I bowled a good deal I was certainly a better bat than a bowler at that time.'

'How did it happen that you took to cricket as a profession?'

'I was very keen on the game and was always longing to play, so when my employer at Goole told me I was getting too old for the work he could find me to do, I thought I would try to earn my living at cricket.'

'What was your first engagement?'

'It was in 1909. I answered an advertisement in the *Athletic News* for a professional at Hawes which is distant only a few miles from the terrible railway catastrophe. To my great surprise I got the job.'

'And at Hawes you began to make your reputation, I suppose?'

'Well, I was pretty successful and headed the bowling averages with 65 wickets at seven and a half runs each.'

'Did you make any big scores for Hawes?'

'No, my highest was 77 against Leyburn but I often played for other clubs and, in one of those matches, I scored 102 for Bedale against Thirsk.'

'I believe you received a trial from the Yorkshire county club?'

'Quite right. That was in 1910. Mr H Arden Crallan, the captain of the Hawes club, who was a fine fast-bowler in his day, recommended me. He also went with me to Harrogate when I was tried. Mr GJV Weigall, the Kent amateur, I remember was in charge but I was evidently not thought much of as I heard nothing further.'

'I believe I am right in saying that Mr Crallan has been a very good friend to you?'

'He has indeed and he still takes a great deal of interest in my doings. He is a fine sportsman and passionately fond of cricket. He also goes in for racing. Perhaps you remember his horse, The Guller, winning the Chester Cup last summer.'

'Over which, doubtless, you won a pile?'

'Sorry to say I didn't. I know nothing about racing and was not even aware till afterwards that the horse was in the race.'

'How came you to qualify for Warwickshire?'

'It was in a rather curious way. Mr Ryder, the secretary to the Warwickshire cricket club, was spending his holidays in Wensleydale during the autumn of 1910 and while playing a round of golf was introduced to Mr Crallan. Naturally, the conversation soon turned upon cricket and my captain strongly recommended me as a likely man for Warwickshire. The result was that I was offered an engagement on the groundstaff at Edgbaston for the season of 1911 and gladly accepted it.'

'For whom did you play during your qualifying stage?'

'The first year I did not get much match cricket and accomplished nothing out of the ordinary but in 1912 I was lent to the Moseley club for Birmingham League games. I was pretty successful for them and scored 106 not out and took six wickets for 38 runs in my first match, which was against Dudley; but I think my best performance that year was 74 not out and seven wickets for 19 runs for the Rest of the League against Walsall, the champions of the year.'

'You played once or twice in first-class cricket before you became properly qualified for Warwickshire, I know?'

'Yes, my first match was against the Australians and though I failed with the bat I captured the wickets of Kelleway and Emery which highly delighted me, the more so since Mr Crallan had journeyed from Yorkshire to witness the game. My first county match was against Worcestershire at Dudley last Whit Monday.'

'Which do you yourself consider your best performances last season?'

'My best innings was undoubtedly my 86 not out against the county of my birth at Birmingham. I don't think I accomplished anything better with the ball than the seven wickets for 34 runs I took against Worcestershire on the same ground.'

'I have heard evidence that you are a big hitter. Can you tell me of anything exceptional that you have done?'

'I don't know about "exceptional". When playing against Northamptonshire, however, I hit Freeman clean over the pavilion at Edgbaston, the ball pitching in the road. I understand the feat has only been accomplished twice before, by PS McDonnell, the Australian, in 1888, and by JH Sinclair, the South African, in 1901.'

'Does slip-fielding suit you?'

'Yes, on the whole, but I like the long field quite as well.'

'No doubt you were quite satisfied with your first season's work?'

'More than satisfied! I simply never dreamed of getting anywhere near 100 wickets. In fact at the commencement of the season I bet one of my colleagues a sovereign that I did not play in more than a dozen county matches! I quite enjoyed handing over that quid!'

'Cricket is not your only game, I know?'

'No, I am very keen indeed on football and play for Stirchley Co-operatives in the Birmingham Wednesday League. Aston Villa asked me to play for the Reserves but I have no wish to take to the game professionally as I think the strain of playing the two games would be too much for me. I also play billiards a good deal. My highest break last winter was 86, the same figure as my highest score for Warwickshire to date.'

'What do you think of first-class cricket as compared to local cricket?'

'I have had so little experience that I hardly care to venture an opinion, but I can easily see that first-class cricket entails a heavy strain on the system, and that one has to keep wonderfully fit to be successful in it. In local cricket one expects to get a wicket every other over but it is more like a case of every hour, or sometimes every day, in county games!

I found this out, especially, when I was struggling for my 100 wickets last August. It took me three matches to get my last five wickets.'

'Were you particularly struck with the play of any of your opponents last summer?'

'I was indeed. Jack Hobbs's innings at Edgbaston and Frank Woolley's batting at Tonbridge I thought were absolutely perfect exhibitions. Among the bowlers I met I found Blythe the most difficult to cope with. We got 16 in our second innings at Tonbridge, you remember.

"Oh yes, I remembered. I made three of them myself, and that was three more than my friend Jeeves made. If it had not been for the great efforts of Parsons and Baker, I should have been top-scorer!"

If Jeeves's ability stood out a mile on the pitch, no less so did his humility in print. Beckoning the 25-year-old was a wonderful career in cricket and a lovely life with Annie.

23.

Aston Villa – Chaos in Albania – Fender reaches his 100 with an all-run six – Warwickshire beat Worcestershire by an innings and 371 runs

AS REVEALED in his interview with Sydney Santall, Percy Jeeves's sporting career almost broadened to include professional football. In an era in which professional sportsmen – and cricketers in particular – were poorly paid, especially out of season, many tried to top up their income by alternating between sports. Such a dual career had been pursued by Warwickshire players before, most notably John Devey who scored 6,515 runs for the Bears between 1887 and 1907, at the same time scoring the goals which powered Aston Villa to five FA Cups and two league titles. Before becoming a regular for England as well as Warwickshire, wicketkeeper Dick Lilley was keen to play football but backed down after secretary R.V. Ryder pointed out the risk of injury.

"I should like to point out that you are by no means robust," Ryder wrote to Lilley in 1892, "and that serious injury is likely to result from your playing football of any sort. I appeal to you strongly to accept my advice and leave the game alone."

Lilley acquiesced to Ryder's request and, two decades later, Jeeves also chose to protect his cricketing future by keeping his football casual – he declined Villa's offer of a contract.

Jeeves entered his second full season amid high expectations. The 1914 edition of *Wisden Cricketers' Almanack* commented in its report on Warwickshire:

> "His first season was nothing short of a triumph. He came out first in bowling with 106 wickets and scored 765 runs with an average of 20. This all-round record suggests tremendous possibilities in the near future. Jeeves is a good punishing bat but it is as a bowler that the Warwickshire people expect most of him. On the fast side of medium pace, he has a very easy action and while fresh he makes the ball come off the ground with plenty of life. Unaccustomed to three-day matches, he was, perhaps, asked to do a little too much bowling, 780 overs. He said himself at the end of the season that, while he was struggling to get his 100 wickets, he fully appreciated the difference between county cricket and ordinary club matches. Whatever may be in store for him, he was, beyond all question, one of the best of the cricketers discovered in 1913."

Wisden editor Sydney H. Pardon considered the rich harvest of young talent emerging around the counties and observed: "It will be disappointing indeed if, to mention only a few names, Lee of Nottinghamshire, Kilner of Yorkshire, Jeeves of Warwickshire, Chester of Worcestershire, R.B. Langden and D.J. Knight do not do a great deal for us in the next few years."

Percy duly acquired a copy of the book – the "cricketers' bible" – and proudly highlighted some of his mentions in pencil.

Jeeves's early-season form suggested that high expectations hung light upon his shoulders. In a friendly for Warwickshire against Moseley at Edgbaston, he dismissed four of the club side's top five, including county team-mates Jack Parsons and George Stephens, then scored 58 not out.

In the championship opener, against Leicestershire at Edgbaston, the 25-year-old took his place in what remains the best quartet of seamers ever to grace a Warwickshire team: title-clinchers Foster and Field, Santall, more than 1,000 first-class wickets behind him, and the potential-laden Jeeves. Foster and Field shared 14 wickets as Leicestershire were thrashed by 258 runs. Jeeves started quietly with 1-36 and 2-31, although the

Post noted that "his fast delivery, introduced almost too rarely, invariably bewildered the batsmen".

Warwickshire travelled next to Bristol where they beat Gloucestershire by ten wickets, an easy victory in which Jeeves again had a supporting role with 1-20 and 2-19. "Jeeves has started somewhat quietly," reported the *Post*, "but, with the support he can now be given in the attack, he ought to improve on last season's record. He will probably prove more destructive when he makes more use of the fast ball which brought him so many victims in 1913."

Warwickshire's strong start left them top of the table but the last week of May brought a by-election in Ipswich, chaos in Albania, severe frosts in Evesham Vale and Foster's men back down to earth with a bump. They were thrashed by an innings and 197 runs by Surrey at The Oval. The brown-hatters, desperate to wrest the title back from Kent, were in command from the opening afternoon when fast bowler John Hitch took 6-74. His wickets included a hat-trick in which Jeeves was the middle victim. Having bowled Tiger Smith with the last ball before tea, Hitch had Jeeves caught behind first ball after the interval, then bowled Willie Hands.

The hat-trick was one of only two interesting passages of a mundane day's play haunted by bad light and showers. The other arrived late when, with Surrey 31 without loss in reply to 226, the last eight balls of the day brought some explosive cricket. Two great players – Frank Foster and Jack Hobbs – did battle. In terrible light, with no sight-screen at the Pavilion End from which Foster was bowling, the odds were stacked heavily against the batsman but Hobbs struck Warwickshire's captain for 16 from three balls, a four sandwiched between two straight sixes into the pavilion. In Stygian gloom, it was almost unbelievable batting.

The spectators were still buzzing at the sight of Foster being roughed up in such breathtaking fashion when Jeeves began the next over by bowling Tom Hayward and Ernie Hayes with successive balls. An immediate appeal against the light was upheld so the bowler slept on a hat-trick.

That feat eluded him on Friday morning when little that Warwickshire attempted met with success. Hobbs advanced imperiously from 34 to 183 (21 fours, one five, two sixes) and then Percy Fender exploited a tiring attack for 140 (25 fours, a five and a six). Surrey piled up 541 against fielders who wilted so badly in the sun that Fender reached his century with an all-run six. Only Jeeves kept some order. On his way to figures of 29-10-109-3 he delivered as many maidens as his colleagues combined, but Warwickshire were outclassed. Second time round they capitulated from 58 without loss to 118 all out, undone by the googlies of William Abel.

Back down to earth indeed but, under Foster, Warwickshire were capable of hitting either end of the form scale at any time. Against Worcestershire at Dudley, they returned to the happy extreme in an amazing match which included two individual feats of a magnitude which any spectator would be grateful to witness once in their lifetime.

The first day, Bank Holiday Monday, brought quiet Warwickshire dominance. A crowd of just over 5,000 saw them bowl Worcestershire out for 188 (Jeeves, returning to the ground on which he made his championship debut, 12-4-27-0) then reply with 122/2. So far, so straightforward.

Next morning, Warwickshire advanced to 197/2 before Parsons, on 102, edged Fred Pearson behind. Foster went in to bat at number five. Four hours and 20 minutes later, the Tipton Road ground was echoing to the cheers of spectators with hands sore from applause. Warwickshire's captain was unbeaten on 305 out of 645/7.

Foster started watchfully. He took 60 minutes to reach 50 and ensure that his team moved well in front. Then his innings steadily gathered momentum. He took a further 45 minutes to reach 100, another 50 to reach 150 and another half an hour to get to 200. That was only the ninth double-century registered for Warwickshire but Foster was far from finished. His fifth 50 came in 35 minutes, his sixth in half an hour as Worcestershire's bowlers met an onslaught of controlled aggression.

There was no slogging, just batting of the highest quality and placement. Foster did not loft a stroke until he was past 150 and struck no sixes, one five, 44 fours, 14 threes, 21 twos and 40 singles.

"There was never anything monotonous in his play and the crowd watched his progress with rapt attention," reported the *Post*. Foster's "remorseless scattering of the Worcestershire fielders over the slopes of the high-perched Dudley ground" left him with the highest score by a Warwickshire player. He added 126 in 85 minutes with Quaife, 60 in 35 with Baker, 40 in 20 with Stephens and 166 in 70 with Smith.

Smith's fall to a return catch by Alf Cliff left the score 594/7 and brought in Percy Jeeves on the threshold of an historic moment. Foster was 268 not out, equal with the highest score by a Warwickshire batsman, Septimus Kinneir against Hampshire at Edgbaston in 1911. Moments later, Kinneir and his team-mates were on their feet cheering as Foster and Jeeves crossed for the record-breaking single. Foster raised his bat to all sides, shook hands with his young team-mate then launched one final, furious assault. Jeeves contributed six (three singles and a three) to an unbroken eighth-wicket stand of 51 in 20 minutes then followed his captain to the pavilion as spectators stood to acclaim Foster. Never before had a batsman scored 300 runs in a day in the County Championship.

It was a day of astounding cricket. Another followed immediately.

Next morning, Worcestershire set out in pursuit of 457 to avoid an innings defeat. Jeeves quickly ousted three of the top four: Fred Bowley, caught at leg slip, Pearson lbw and Cliff, who played on. "Jeeves started in deadly fashion," reported the *Post*, "and, exploiting new tactics with a strong field on the leg-side, soon shattered any hope that Worcestershire would avoid an innings defeat." Then, at 85/4, Jeeves was replaced by Field.

Seventeen years had elapsed since Field made his county debut and 39 since he entered the world in Weethley Hamlet, a tiny settlement in a bulge on the western fringe of Warwickshire, jutting into Worcestershire. If Field had been born a few hundred yards in any of three directions his hundreds of wickets would have been taken for Worcestershire. Now, more than ever, they regretted that quirk of geography.

Field began with a maiden. Bertie Stevens scored two from the second ball of his second over, leaving the bowler's figures: 1.2-0-2-0. But, according to the *Post,* "from the first over it was very obvious to the spectators that Field's deliveries were dangerous to an unusual degree".

The veteran bowled faster than ever and whipped the ball back off the seam. Such a delivery uprooted Stevens's leg stump. Another, next ball, forced William Taylor to play on and left Worcestershire 108/6 at lunch.

The 45-minute interval did nothing to quench Field's fire. Straight afterwards, Maurice Foster, having defied for 51, was bowled, only to be reprieved by a shout of "no ball". The next delivery reared off a length and Foster fended back a return catch. Richard Burrows fell in similar fashion, Ernie Bale's stumps were shattered and when Arthur Conway was lbw, first ball, Field had taken six wickets for no runs in 44 balls. His overall figures: 8.4-7-2-6.

Jeeves (16-2-30-3) had prepared the way for his team-mate by taking out the top order but Warwickshire's whopping win, by an innings and 321 runs, was assured immortal fame by the brilliance of Frank Rowbotham Foster and Ernest Frank Field.

24.

Leg-theory – Warner is non-plussed – A sticky dog – Almost unplayable

FRANK FIELD'S destruction of Worcestershire was principally down to speed. Frank Foster and Percy Jeeves were not as fast as Field but were brisk enough and also busy working on a new strategy. Both men lacked Field's mighty physique but were able to generate considerable pace from the wicket – and this was an ability Foster was keen to exploit.

Almost 20 years were to elapse before England's deployment of leg-theory or "Bodyline" (bowling at the batsman to force catches into the close leg-side field) in an Ashes series in Australia would almost tear the international cricket world apart, but it was a tactic which Foster and Jeeves were already deploying in the county game. They did so the day after Worcestershire were crushed at Dudley, against Middlesex at Edgbaston, though it was with orthodox bowling that Jeeves left a big impression on England captain and selector Plum Warner.

Warwickshire batted first and made 361, Jeeves striking 43 in 55 minutes – "an admirable display of enterprising batting". When Middlesex began their reply in fading light at 6.05pm, Field's 6-2 at Dudley failed to earn him the new ball. Foster and Jeeves took it and, the *Post* reported, "the Warwickshire captain pleased his admirers by setting his field to take full advantage of his leg-ball". Middlesex's openers both soon fell, Foster dismissing William Robertson while Jeeves's sixth delivery had Frank Tarrant caught in the slips.

After Middlesex struggled to 15/2 in 13 overs of leg-theory, Foster threw the ball to Field. 'Big Frank' marked out his run as 6,000 spectators roared for their hero to carry on where he left off the day before. Unsurprisingly, Middlesex were not so keen, especially with Warner having suffering a groin strain in the field. An immediate appeal against the light was upheld.

On the second day, 'Patsy' Hendren soon chipped Foster into the leg-trap while Jeeves bowled with a short leg, short fine leg, short square leg, mid-on and extra mid-on until rain arrived to wash out play after lunch. When Middlesex resumed, on the final day, on 139/3, 222 behind, the match was already doomed to stalemate but when their ninth wicket fell at 283, there was still something to play for – three points for the first-innings lead in a draw. So, rather than declare, Warner limped out to join Arthur Littlejohn.

Warwickshire decided that Warner was good enough to deal with leg-theory so plumped for old-fashioned virtues of pitching the ball up and hitting the seam. Jeeves was good at that.

He tormented the England captain. Twice, on seven and ten, Warner edged but Parsons dropped catches in the cordon. The tenth-wicket pair ground out 53 before the England captain, on 20, was defeated yet again by Jeeves, this time terminally. Beaten by a series of exquisite leg-cutters, Warner got one that went the other way and his middle stump landed halfway back to Tiger Smith. The bowler's tidy but unspectacular figures, 28.2-7-43-2, disguised his toying with one of England's finest batsmen.

There was just time for Foster to open the innings with a merry 51 in 15 minutes, the fastest half-century in county cricket, in which he lifted Littlejohn twice into the pavilion and twice over the covered stand, but it was the name Jeeves which had been inked firmly into Warner's notebook.

Two days later the return match began at Lord's and Jeeves again left his mark. Tarrant, a hard-hitting batsman, was enjoying the season of his life but was, according to the *Post*, "completely baffled by a ball from Jeeves which upset his stumps instead of going away to the off".

The batsman did have 95, mind you, an innings which set up a ten-wicket win. Tarrant also contributed 7/31 in Warwickshire's second innings and rounded off the match with three wickets in an over, watched by Jeeves from the non-striker's end. Having been 63 all out at Lord's a year earlier, Warwickshire this time folded for 69.

Feckless in 1913, this time Foster's men had been trapped on a drying wicket and, throughout the damp summer, the conditions afforded batsmen some mitigation for low scores. Derbyshire arrived next at Edgbaston to find a horrible 'sticky dog' and were bowled out for 71 by Foster (6-18) and Field (4-36). In the second innings, the younger men did the damage. Harry Howell, a promising footballer on the books of Wolverhampton Wanderers as an inside-right, took 6/31 and Jeeves 4/32 as Derbyshire made 127. Howell bowled with real pace while the *Post* reported that "Jeeves, aided by the wind, made his fast delivery almost unplayable".

He was keen for it to stay that way because two days later came a very special fixture – Yorkshire away, at the Savile Town ground in Dewsbury, a hefty six-hit from where he spent the first 13 years of his life.

25.

Jeeves returns to his roots – Quaife bores 3,307 paying spectators – Assassination in Sarajevo – A bail is carried 41 paces

AS YORKSHIRE'S outground at Dewsbury was just a couple of miles up the hill from Percy Jeeves's birthplace at Earlsheaton, his return to his roots as a rising star of English cricket attracted much attention.

"Yorkshire and Warwickshire will meet in a three days match at Savile Town next week, starting on Monday at noon," reported the *Dewsbury Times*. "Warwickshire's visit should be especially attractive, for one of their team is Percy Jeeves of Earlsheaton, described in the daily press as 'a coming player'."

The county team's annual visit to the ground always drew good crowds and, for the Warwickshire game, the attendance was further boosted by good weather. High up on Park Road, the field was susceptible to biting winds and playing and watching cricket there was an unforgiving business on a cold day. But for the return of Jeeves, the venue was blessed by sunshine. The first two days were attended by big crowds – 3,307 and 3,902 paying spectators, as well as many more members.

Warwickshire dominated the match but had to settle for a draw after a defiant rearguard action by the home side. The Bears seized control on the first day thanks to a sparkling 206 from Crowther Charlesworth. The affable Lancastrian was a popular man and known in this neck of the woods from when he used to play club cricket at nearby Armitage Bridge. As a batsman, he loved to attack and, after taking 85 minutes to score his first 50, required only another 35 to add his second, then grew more aggressive as he went along.

"It was a bold and adventurous innings which delighted and refreshed all who saw it," reported the *Dewsbury Times*. When Charlesworth finally fell, having struck a chanceless 206 (230 minutes, 27 fours, two sixes) out of 283 runs added while he was at the crease, he was cheered back to the pavilion even by Yorkshire's partisan followers.

Quaife added a sedate 63 ("the little man certainly was a bore but he played his own game well" noted the local paper) while Jeeves went into bat to a warm ovation after tea and ended the day unbeaten on 20. "Much interest naturally centred on Jeeves, the Earlsheaton lad," reported the *Dewsbury Times*. "His form with the bat, in late afternoon, was none too convincing and Hirst might have snapped him from a hot return but he stopped the ball with his wrist instead of the palm of his hand." Warwickshire closed the day on 353/6.

On Tuesday morning, Jeeves added ten to his tally before clipping Rhodes into the hands of Sir Archibald White at mid-on. The Bears declared on 424/8, to which the home crowd expected their team to respond with a hefty total of their own. But Yorkshire's stellar, if ageing, line-up mustered only 262. Jeeves took 3-54, dismissing Wilfred Rhodes, Alonzo Drake and Tom Birtles, and "proved himself a useful type of right-hand bowler such as his native county could find room for" according to the *Yorkshire Post*. The follow-on was enforced just before the close, at which the hosts were 2/1 with Sir Archibald already out, bowled by Willie Hands.

Yorkshire needed to bat for most of Wednesday to save the game and they succeeded, assisted by the absence from the field of Frank Foster. The captain was out of sorts having enjoyed the hospitality of the White Rose the previous night. Foster bowled only five overs without taking a wicket and the rest of the bowlers could not compensate for his indiscipline. David Denton scored 88 and Rhodes 75, enabling Sir Archibald to declare at 345/9, leaving a notional target of 184 in an hour and a half after tea.

The Bears finished on 83/4 but the crowd at least saw their local favourite bat again when Jeeves was sent in at number three for a hit. He managed only ten before sending up a catch off Rhodes.

From Dewsbury, Warwickshire headed to the Bulls Head Ground in Binley Road, Coventry, where Charlesworth followed his double century against Yorkshire with 115 against Gloucestershire. The visitors were beaten by an innings and 197 runs after Howell and Jeeves again dovetailed devastatingly. In the second innings, Howell took 6-34 while Jeeves ended with 4-47 and "bowled far better than his figures suggest".

"So powerful was the onslaught of the two young bowlers," added the *Birmingham Daily Post*, "that Gloucestershire had a bad attack of nerves. Not one of the 11, not even G.L. Jessop, ever timed the ball with any degree of accuracy and the 94 runs they collected were largely by means of strokes beyond the pale of classification."

Jeeves ended the match already on 29 wickets for the season at 20.27 each and should have added the great Jessop to his list of illustrious victims. But when the 'Croucher', on eight, skied to point, Quaife missed the catch before offering the age-old mitigation – "the sun was in my eyes".

After playing on 18 days out of 21, Warwickshire at last entered a welcome ten-day break before they faced Lancashire at Edgbaston. While the Bears took a breather, there was excitement in Goole as the King and Queen passed through on the way to Hull. The tennis at Wimbledon was rain-affected but, in a fourth round thriller, Edgbaston-born Arthur Holden Lowe was edged out 6-3, 6-4, 5-7, 10-8 by German opponent Otto Froitzheim.

Arthur Conway's 9-38 propelled Worcestershire to victory over Gloucestershire in the only championship match ever played at Moreton-in-Marsh, Frank Woolley scored a century at Ashby-de-la-Zouch and, on the eighth day of their break, Warwickshire's thoughts were turning to the Lancashire game. Septimus Kinneir's thoughts, in particular. He had chosen the match for his benefit, so he picked the team.

The game began on Wednesday 29 June and, to Kinneir's satisfaction, 3,944 people paid for admission, generating receipts of £103 9s to which a bucket collection added £19 1s 4d for the beneficiary.

As always, newspaper sellers circulated the ground during play and spectators who purchased a local paper were able to peruse a long match preview. The piece detailed Lancashire's powerful batting, led by the masterful Johnny Tyldesley. Those who also turned to the news pages, meanwhile, came across the headline: "Assassination of Austrian Archduke – Dastardly crime in Bosnian town." No one watching the young man in the middle, busy working his way through Lancashire's top order, could possibly have imagined that the incident chronicled in print before them would trigger a catastrophic sequence of events that would cost that bowler his life.

In reply to Warwickshire's 222, Lancashire reached 47 without loss before Jeeves trapped the obdurate Harry Makepeace lbw. That brought in Tyldesley, a habitual plunderer of Warwickshire, but in the same over he was sent on his way by "a very fine delivery that came back, upset the leg-stump and carried the bail 41 paces". Jeeves also had Jack Sharp caught behind and Bill Tyldesley taken by Foster at second slip. Next morning, he added the wicket of Bill Huddlestone to finish with 32-11-75-5, a superb effort in hot weather against strong opposition on a good batting pitch.

After Warwickshire set the Red Rose 283 to win on the final day, Jeeves should have had Tyldesley early again but the batsman, on eight, was dropped by Smith. The error cost the Bears victory as Tyldesley survived to make a fighting 38 while all collapsed around him. Lancashire were hanging on at 100/9 (Foster 14-5-19-5, Jeeves 13-6-15-0) when rain arrived to save them.

That rain set in for the week and ruined the next match, against Sussex at Nuneaton. The second day brought no cricket at all but some news which brought smiles to Warwickshire's dressing room and supporters. Percy Jeeves and Jack Parsons had been selected to play for the Players against the Gentlemen at The Oval the following week.

The Gentlemen v Players (amateurs v professionals) matches were the showpiece occasions of the English season. All the top players featured in them with counties obliged to release their stars for games usually played at Lord's or The Oval but also sometimes at festival venues such as Scarborough and Hastings. Especially in those years, like 1914, when no Test matches were scheduled, the Gents v Players games were highlights of the cricketing summer, so this recognition for the two young Bears was thrilling for them and the county club.

There was nothing thrilling about the Sussex match as it drifted to a draw. On the final day, Sussex declared their second innings at 102/1 from 46 overs of batting which was "stodgy to the point of boredom". With the contest stone dead, Foster and Jeeves opened the batting to try to give the crowd some entertainment. Wicketkeeper George Street and medium-pacer Henry Roberts opened the bowling and delivered 15.3 overs in half an hour. Jeeves was bowled by Roberts for five before Street dismissed Foster, Charlesworth and Howell. They proved to be the only three wickets of Street's career which was to be ended early in 1924 when, aged 35, he was killed in a motor cycling accident.

Before the big match at The Oval, Jeeves had one more county assignment, against Hampshire at Edgbaston, and he warmed up nicely with another five-wicket haul in a six-wicket victory. The leg-trap was working well as Jeeves and Foster shared 18 wickets. They took five each in the second innings, Jeeves bowling hardly a loose ball in 22.2-9-33-5.

Despite interruptions by rain, the match was over at 3.28pm on the final day after Hampshire agreed to play on in drizzle because everybody needed to get on the road: Hampshire to Bristol to face Gloucestershire, Warwickshire to Hastings to play against Sussex – and Jeeves and Parsons to London.

26.

The finest cricketers in the world – Gunn tests the crowd's patience – A brute of a delivery – Jeeves is the talk of English cricket

IN JULY 1907, Percy Jeeves walked down the hill from Luddington Station in the Marshland countryside to find a pitch barely discernible from the rest of the meadow, ready for an afternoon of archetypal village cricket. In July 1914, Jeeves walked through the grand gates at The Oval and entered the Players' dressing room to rub shoulders with the finest cricketers in the world in one of the most important matches of the year.

Most of the team in which Jeeves and Jack Parsons took their places were already established as giants of the Golden Age. Under captain John Hitch was a wonderful batting unit led by Surrey's own Jack Hobbs and including Frank Tarrant and Jack Hearne of Middlesex, George Gunn of Nottinghamshire and Frank Woolley of Kent. The middle and lower orders comprised London and West Midlands stock: Hitch, Ernie Hayes and Bert Strudwick were on home ground at The Oval while Jeeves and Parsons were joined by Fred Bowley of Worcestershire. Jeeves knew all his team-mates to some degree except Gunn, Warwickshire having not recently played Nottinghamshire.

The amateurs, captained by C.B. Fry, were weakened by Foster's decision to lead Warwickshire at Hastings. The Bears skipper's preference for county duty irritated the London press and deprived spectators of the fascinating prospect of Foster and Jeeves facing each other, but the Gentlemen still boasted a formidable top order. After openers Reg Spooner (Lancashire) and Doug Robinson

(Gloucestershire) came three towering figures: Fry (Sussex), Plum Warner (Middlesex) and Gilbert Jessop (Gloucestershire). In the middle order were Percy Fender (Surrey) and Michael Falcon (Norfolk and an MCC regular but not connected to a first-class county) while four bowlers – Frank Mann (Middlesex), Ernest Kirk (Surrey), Jack White (Somerset) and Arthur Jaques (Hampshire) – joined the fixture for the first time.

The morning of 9 July dawned damp in south London but the clouds soon gave way to watery sunshine and play began on time. Hitch won the toss and chose to bat, so Jeeves watched the opening exchanges from the balcony. Eight thousand spectators saw the Gents make a strong start. On a fast pitch, Tarrant fended to short leg and Hearne sliced to point. When Hobbs was caught at mid-on the Players were 12/3.

Gunn and Woolley saw off the new ball and took their side to 84/3 at lunch. Woolley was then yorked by Falcon for 78 (eight fours, seven threes) but Gunn tested the crowd's patience by taking two hours to reach 50 and then adding only four more runs in the next half an hour. There was much relief among the spectators when the Nottinghamshire blocker edged Kirk to the wicketkeeper.

Parsons was the first of the Warwickshire players to get in and he looked nervous. He required two streaky boundaries to reach 24 before he was bowled by White. At 181/7, Jeeves went in to join a familiar face at the crease. Bowley was usually a rival and had been at the wicket when Jeeves bowled his first ball in championship cricket at Dudley, 14 months earlier, but now the Midlands pair added 15, with Jeeves making the 11 runs he required to pass 1,000 in first-class cricket, before he was bowled by Jaques.

At 205/9, an untidy innings needed a late fillip and it arrived in the form of a spectacular assault on the bowling by last pair Hitch and Strudwick. They thrashed 122 in 65 minutes to lift the Players to 327 and leave the Gents five overs to face before the close. Jeeves bowled two of those and Hitch three but Spooner and Robinson defended vigilantly to take the score to five without loss. The first day closed with Jeeves having played a peripheral role – an extra on the big stage. But on the second morning he was central to the Players seizing control.

In overcast conditions, the opening stand reached 60 before Jeeves was recalled to the attack and unfurled a brilliant spell. He immediately unleashed a devilish off-cutter to ruin Robinson's stumps and bring in Fry. Jeeves's first ball to the captain was a perfectly pitched leg-cutter which was edged, only for Hayes to fumble in the slips. Jeeves found the edge of Spooner's bat, then Fry's again, but, to astonishment from players and spectators alike, both times Woolley failed in the cordon. That was exceptionally unlucky for the bowler – Woolley took 1,018 catches during his first-class cricket career and dropped very little.

For an hour, the Warwickshire bowler was almost unplayable yet he ended the innings with just one wicket – 13.2-3-24-1 – after Hitch torpedoed the Gents with a post-lunch burst of 5-16 in 28 balls. Jeeves had made his mark though.

After the Gents were all out for 237, the Players, leading by 90, built their advantage carefully after tea. Hobbs, reining himself in, took 110 minutes to reach 50 and was on 79 at the close with his side 143/3 – 233 in front.

To have Hobbs not out overnight guaranteed a big crowd next morning and spectators flocked to The Oval on Friday in anticipation of their hero filling his boots. They were not disappointed. But their reflections at close of play were to dwell appreciatively upon the skills of two men – John Berry Hobbs and Percy Jeeves.

Hobbs adorned the morning session with divine drives on his way to 156 before, in search of his 22nd four, he aimed to leg off Kirk and was bowled. His wicket triggered a declaration which left the Gentlemen 393 to win. It was a tall target but, on a good wicket, saving the match looked within the compass of a batting line-up of their calibre. A fascinating contest beckoned and the crowd, 6,000-strong in the morning, grew considerably after lunch.

The Gents started positively. Eight runs came from the first over from Hitch and they reached 35 without loss. Then Hitch switched Jeeves to the Pavilion End and the bowler produced another brilliant spell which this time was rewarded with wickets. Robinson was lured into a drive and the captain clung on at slip; 35/1. Jeeves straightened Spooner up and had him caught behind off a brute of a delivery; 42/2. Fry fell the same way; 45/3. Warner, still to score, edged but survived as the ball fell just short of the cordon.

This renowned top order's torment at the hands of Jeeves was only ended by the abrasive Kirk who hit him out of the attack with three fours in an over. But Kirk's resistance was soon terminated by Tarrant and the Gents were well-beaten. Falcon, who defied for 50 minutes for 17, later recounted to Warwickshire secretary Rowland Ryder his "vivid memories of Jeeves's deliveries biting into the soft pitch and throwing up pieces of turf – I said: 'Hullo, here's someone'".

At 4.10pm, Jeeves applied the finishing touch by bowling Jaques to seal victory by 241 runs. He shook hands with Jaques (commiserating with the batsman was a courtesy he had learned from Frank Field who never gloated at a victim's demise) before accepting the congratulations of his team-mates. Jeeves had won the match for his team with figures of 15-3-44-4 so led the Players back into the pavilion. The Warwickshire player was first up the pavilion steps, before Hobbs, Woolley, Gunn, Hitch – great players following in his wake.

"There was no player on either side who created a more profound impression than Jeeves," commented the *Post*. It was no cheap, parochial praise. Jeeves had announced himself as one of the very best.

The boy who once rode the light railway home from Luddington with his pals, full of untapped potential, boarded the train back from London to Birmingham as the talk of English cricket.

27.

Four wickets in four balls – "Armies mobilising" – Jeeves and Foster in deadly tandem – War is declared

THE GENTS v Players fixture was discharged in its usual genteel fashion as English cricket and English life chugged along largely unaware of the cataclysm which lurked around the corner. Some spectators at The Oval, not least the politicians who liked to pop in during breaks in parliamentary business, discussed overseas matters. But, while the newspapers documented an increasingly volatile situation in the Balkans, few people seriously believed that peace in wider Europe was in jeopardy. For most, life continued as normal.

Normal, in this soggy summer, meant rain which sentenced Warwickshire's next three matches to draws. From the spotlight of The Oval, Percy Jeeves headed to the backwater of Northampton. He arrived placed tenth in the national bowling averages, with 47 wickets at 18.87 each, and soon reached 50. He took 3-61 in the first innings and also felled top-scorer William Wells with a painful blow over the heart from a ball that reared off a length. Jeeves had a hand in each of Northamptonshire's first six wickets.

"Jeeves's fielding at third slip was brilliant," reported the *Post*. "In that position he caught the two Dentons and Smith while off his own bowling he had Haywood and Thompson caught at extra mid-off and caught-and-bowled Woolley."

Next day he struck 27, including three successive fours off medium-pacer William East, before the match petered out on the final afternoon. Septimus Kinneir and Billy Quaife shut up shop, rather prematurely, felt some spectators who let forth "frequent ebullitions of dissatisfaction in the form of ironical cheering".

The return fixture at Edgbaston was also rain-affected but what cricket was possible did throw up a piece of history. On the final afternoon, play began at 2.45pm. The match was stone dead and Warwickshire reached 101/5, with Jeeves at the non-striker's end, when Trinidadian slow left-armer Sydney Smith began his 18th over. To the fourth ball, the left-handed Charles Baker leaned forward and was caught at short leg by George Thompson. In went 20-year-old Arthur Foster (Frank's brother, a man of no cricketing ability, bizarrely selected for his only county match). He was right-handed so Thompson moved to slip. Foster duly edged his first ball there. Next in was Harry Howell. Thompson returned to short leg, Howell popped up a catch and Smith had a hat-trick, all caught by the same fielder.

The bowler had not finished. After Jeeves played out a maiden, Field skied the first ball of the next over to mid-off to supply a fourth wicket in four balls for the West Indian.

Next came a visit to Leicestershire at Hinckley and a drawn match ravaged by rain and gales. "The large marquee occupied by pressmen was blown in for a moment or two," reported the *Post*. "Some of the journalists within were in danger of being seriously hurt by falling poles but this unpleasant experience was avoided and the only disaster entailed was the loss of innumerable papers which strewed all parts of the playing surface."

The loss of reporters' notes that windy Saturday did not really constitute too much of a disaster but the threat of true disaster was escalating. During the weekend, newspaper coverage of the situation in Europe expanded considerably. "Now Russia and Germany may be involved, Armies mobilising" and "Europe on the brink of a great war" were the grave headlines in the *Post*. On 30 July Prime Minister Herbert Asquith told the House of Commons: "I can only usefully say that the Government are not reducing their efforts to do everything in their power to circumscribe the area of possible conflict." War was imminent, but could it be contained?

To this alarming and confusing backdrop, county cricket continued. Warwickshire travelled north to Lancashire for the first championship match ever to be played at Lune Road, Lancaster. Overlooked by gasometers and flanked by the railway, the ground sat beside the river with its incessant traffic. With all the neighbourhood noise and fumes, Jeeves could have been back at the Pleasure Grounds in Goole.

In London, frantic efforts continued to avert war. In Lancaster, spectators enjoyed a wonderful day's cricket. The weather was perfect and the play engrossing.

After choosing to bat, Warwickshire raced to 60 without loss then slumped to 96/4 at lunch before Billy Quaife and Charles Baker rebuilt in contrasting styles.

The former dropped anchor, at one stage scoring seven in 70 minutes, while his partner attacked. Baker hit medium-pacer Bill Huddlestone over the railway into the river on his way to 103 out of a partnership of 150.

Another collapse followed including the wicket of Jeeves, out for three, and Quaife was on 87 when last man Field went in. The tail-ender refrained from his customary hit-or-bust strategy to give his fellow professional a chance to reach his century. Quaife shed his caution to lift Harry Dean for six and reached his ton in the next over, to generous applause. The spectators had thoroughly enjoyed a lovely day of fine, fluctuating cricket.

On Friday, in reply to 346, Lancashire's batting, the pride of the county, was blown away by Foster and Jeeves. There was no leg-theory, just magnificent straight fast bowling with the stumps hit nine times. Foster ousted numbers one, two and four, Bill Tyldesley, Makepeace and Sharp, while Jeeves, bowling into the wind, castled Johnny and Ernest Tyldesley, had James Heap caught by Howell, then bowled Whitehead and Huddlestone with successive balls and finally Dean to end the innings.

Lancashire were all out for 128; Foster 17-1-58-4, Jeeves 16.3-4-51-6. After his match-winning spell for the Players at The Oval, Jeeves's name had been noted around the country and now the cricket-lovers of Lancaster joined his list of admirers. Despite his Yorkshire roots, they applauded him warmly, even though he had bowled their team into a near-hopeless position.

Lancashire trailed by 218 but, Foster and Jeeves having just bowled all but two overs in the first innings, the captain declined to enforce the follow-on. This decision was appreciated by the home club who were keen to take revenue from a third day's play.

On that final day Lancashire, set 361, made only 187, Foster and Jeeves sharing another six wickets to each finish with eight in the match. It was wonderful bowling by two men close to the peak of their powers. But it was the last time they would ever play in a game which was free of interference from war.

By the time Warwickshire's team arrived back in Birmingham, Germany was at war with France and Russia. Foreign Secretary Sir Edward Grey warned that, if the German fleet entered the North Sea or English Channel, Britain would respond vigorously. His warning was unheeded. Within 72 hours, Britain too was at war.

28.

Chapman is commissioned to buy horses – "Your Country Needs You" – 'Punter' Humphries is completely baffled – Jeeves and Jaques

COUNTY CRICKET continued despite the declaration of war but, during the next round of matches, starting on Bank Holiday Monday 3 August, teams began to be depleted and matches commensurately devalued. Against Essex at Derby, Derbyshire lost leading batsman John Chapman who, the *Post* reported, "fielded during the morning but was called away by the War Office in the afternoon, having been commissioned to buy horses". Without him, Derbyshire were all out for 31 and 94.

In the Roses match at Old Trafford, Lancashire were deprived of their captain when "in the course of the afternoon, Mr A.H. Hornby was called up by the War Office in connection with the purchase of remounts and immediately left the ground for home to receive instructions. Sir Archibald White, the Yorkshire captain, and Mr R.H. Spooner are also expected to be called up".

For Worcestershire's visit to Edgbaston, Warwickshire remained at full strength but, though the visitors began that way, they were reduced to nine men after the second day when brothers Geoffrey and Neville Foster were "called away to fulfil military duties". Their departures spoiled the game as substitutes Charles Collier and Arthur Conway were not allowed to bat. Although Warwickshire were closing in on an unlikely victory late on the last day of the rain-affected match, everyone was pleased that rain returned before they could defeat heavily disadvantaged opponents.

The Bears' winning position had been forced by Jeeves whose opening-day analysis of 7-52 included another five victims clean bowled. From the City End, the *Post* observed, "varying his attack with great judgement he was most successful with a ball that whipped back but managed to get a surprising degree of pace out of the pitch". Worcestershire were all out for 122.

Rain permitted only 75 minutes of play on the second day but the 4,000 spectators were at least cheered briefly when, during a bright spell in the afternoon, Foster, Jeeves, Hands and Howell ventured out for a spot of fielding practice. "This commendable move was watched with keen interest and provoked frequent outbursts of enthusiasm," commented the *Post*.

On the final day, play did not begin until 4pm. Warwickshire resumed their first innings on 82/4 and advanced to 139, securing three points for a first-innings lead. Worcestershire then went back in with less than an hour's play left but, with only nine men eligible to bat, hit deep trouble as they lurched to 7/4. Foster started with seven successive maidens and Jeeves opened up with 8-4-7-2 but, to relief all round, another downpour at 6pm ended the match.

With war underway, Warwickshire's committee considered abandoning the season but decided, in common with the other counties, that to do so would achieve little. Indeed, they continued to plan for the following season and accepted offers from Essex and Nottinghamshire to resume fixtures with them in 1915. In the immediate term, next came a home game against familiar opposition. Yorkshire were on a roll of six successive wins and, even without captain Sir Archibald, comfortably made it seven. They were victorious by 163 runs, despite Jeeves taking 4-67 in their first innings and hitting a "vigorous" 22.

The following day's *Post* contained its usual detailed report of play at Edgbaston. On the front page, meanwhile, was a strident and foreboding plea. On 8 August, the paper's many thousands of readers read: "YOUR KING AND COUNTRY NEEDS YOU – a call to arms – An addition of 100,000 men to His Majesty's regular army is immediately necessary. Terms of Service: General service for a period of three years or until the war is concluded. Age of enlistment between 19 and 30.

"HOW TO JOIN: full information can be obtained at any post office in the kingdom OR at any military depot. GOD SAVE THE KING."

The Call to Arms was enthusiastically received. Enlistment in Birmingham was heavy with long queues forming at recruiting offices despite torrential rain. Jeeves was determined to do his patriotic duty but was contracted to play out the cricket season for the county. Four games remained and Warwickshire intended to fulfil them.

Their visit to Derby went ahead despite Derbyshire having lost Chapman and captain Richard Baggallay to the army. On a wet pitch, 20 wickets fell on the first day. Frank Foster and Sydney Santall took five each to bowl the home side out for 122 before Warwickshire replied with 126, Jeeves top-scoring with 36. Next day, Jeeves took 4-35 as Derbyshire folded again. Foster then smashed 48 in 25 minutes to hurry his side to a six-wicket win. Poor batting conditions contributed to the brevity of the match but applying one's mind to batting was difficult when family, friends and colleagues were on the way to war.

That match was over in a day and a half. The next was concluded in a day and an hour. When Kent visited Edgbaston, 30 wickets fell in the first three sessions. Warwickshire were bowled out for 111 by 22-year-old leg-spinner Percy 'Tich' Freeman, whose 7-25 unveiled a talent which was to bring him 3,776 first-class wickets at 18.42 over the next 22 years. Kent then looked set for a useful lead at 106/6, with David Jennings and Lionel Troughton building a partnership, but they were separated by some Jeeves magic.

"A brilliant bit of fielding turned the tide," the *Post* recorded. "A ball from Jeeves was cut in the direction of point and the batsmen started to run. The bowler dashed headlong for the ball, however, and in one movement picked it up and threw the wicket down, Jennings dropping his bat in the crease a second too late."

In the same over, Jeeves bowled Colin Blythe and Arthur Fielder for ducks to send Kent tumbling towards 111 all out.

With the scores level on first innings, the Bears then came a cropper against a bowler called Fielder. The veteran paceman took 7-34 to rattle Warwickshire out for 78. Kent coasted to a nine-wicket win on the second morning, despite the early loss of Punter Humphries "completely baffled by a ball which pitched leg and hit off" from Jeeves.

Printed alongside cricket scores in the papers now, however, were casualty reports from the war. The British Expeditionary Force was sustaining heavy losses and cricket was starting to appear frivolous and irrelevant as the conflict escalated. Surrey lost use of The Oval to the military and MCC decided to have no cricket at Lord's in September.

The traditional end-of-season Champion County v Rest of England match was cancelled.

Warwickshire's next game, against Hampshire at Northlands Road, attracted small crowds. Hampshire won by four wickets after one of Jeeves's quietest matches; he scored six and four and took 1-81 and 0-20. The stand-out performance came from Hampshire leg-spinner Arthur Jaques who took 7-51 as his team closed in on victory.

Like Jeeves, Jaques was soon to join up. Two young men, whose lives began within two days of each other in March 1888 and went on to grace the cricket fields of England, would soon lose those lives in the muddy hell of the Western Front.

29.

Jeeves bats brilliantly – Jeeves bowls brilliantly – Jeeves fields brilliantly – Jeeves joins up

FROM SOUTHAMPTON, Warwickshire made the short journey to Kent for their last away game of the season at the Bat and Ball Ground in Gravesend. It was a venue at which Kent loved playing – they had won their last 11 matches there, most recently by nine wickets over a much-weakened Somerset side. Despite the war, Kent were able to select a strong team while also giving a debut to 19-year-old Clifton College schoolboy George Whitehead.

After Kent chose to bat on a damp pitch, opening batsman Whitehead, a player of huge potential, was one of 20 wickets to fall on the first day. He was out for five, edging Frank Foster behind to become one of four victims for Warwickshire's captain as the home side were dismissed for 167.

Jeeves enjoyed no luck with the ball but then lifted Warwickshire to 179 with an innings of breathtaking audacity. One of the best bowling attacks ever to represent Kent or, indeed, any county – Arthur Fielder, Colin Blythe, Tich Freeman and Frank Woolley – was thumped to all parts. Going in at 72/5 on a difficult pitch, "Jeeves completely changed the appearance of affairs" reported the *Post*. "Driving with immense power he hit two sixes and eight fours in a brilliant 61 in 50 minutes."

Jeeves and Willie Hands smashed 59 in 25 minutes but the pyrotechnics came in a losing cause. Second time round, Warwickshire were unpicked for 99 by Fielder (4-10) and Woolley (4-38) and their 99-run defeat was sealed at 5.05pm on the second day.

Earlier than planned, the Bears returned to Birmingham. As the war clouds thickened, their thoughts on the journey home centred less upon the match just finished and more upon whatever might lay ahead – beyond the cricket season and far beyond cricket.

They had one more match to play, against Surrey. In normal circumstances, with Surrey crowned champions, beaten only once all year and with all their famous personnel selected, the match would have supplied a wonderful climax to the season. But the opening day attracted only 2,500 people and the atmosphere was moribund. Everybody knew this was the last match of the season. But the last for how long? Nobody knew. Jeeves, in his 50th first-class game, simply seized the opportunity to play wonderfully well one more time.

His contribution to Warwickshire's 177 was small but quirky. Six of his seven runs came from one smite over square leg off Razor Smith before he perished hit wicket for the only time in his career, disturbing his own bails from a ball by medium-pacer Tom Rushby. Then he tore through the champions' illustrious top order.

Hayward, "all at sea", was bowled for two. Jack Hobbs, fresh from striking a glorious 266 against Nottinghamshire at The Oval, reached 16 then received "a ball which swung across and hit leg stump". Ducat edged one that went the other way. On the second morning, Warwickshire were weakened by the loss of Colin Langley who left to report to his regiment, but Jeeves added the wickets of Bert Strudwick and John Hitch to finish with 19-4-52-5 – his 12th five-for in first-class cricket.

The final act of the season at Edgbaston was Surrey's pursuit of a target of 211 in a day and a session. After tea on Friday, Warwickshire bowled superbly as the champions ground to 81/3 by the close. Jeeves yet again bowled Hayward while Field removed Hobbs for just 17.

On the final morning, Andy Ducat played on to Jeeves then Percy Fender and Ernie Hayes defended stubbornly until their partnership was broken in spectacular fashion. When Jeeves bowled to Hayes "a short run was attempted and picking up the ball smoothly the bowler took deliberate aim and hit the stumps. Hayes, who answered Fender's call, crossed and sacrificed his wicket in favour of the amateur. It was wonderfully cool work on the part of Jeeves".

Surrey's last seven wickets fell for 46 in an hour as Warwickshire finished the season triumphantly with an 80-run victory. Foster took 5-48 while Jeeves's 2-36 gave him match figures of 7-88, plus a splendid run-out. The two all-rounders had outclassed the champions and they left the Edgbaston field to loud cheers. Foster had done the double, having passed 1,000 runs and 100 wickets in the season. Jeeves had taken 85 wickets at 19.50 each. He was, according to the *Wisden* correspondent, "perhaps one of the great bowlers of the future".

But as the two men stepped through the picket gate and climbed the pavilion steps in the Saturday morning sunshine they departed first-class cricket forever.

With the season over, Jeeves had much to discuss and not just with Edwin and Nancy up in Goole. According to Rowland Ryder, in his book *Cricket Calling,* Percy had popped the question. "Percy Jeeves," wrote Ryder, "became engaged to Annie Austin, younger sister of George Austin, the Warwickshire scorer."

Census records reveal that Annie was somewhat older than Jeeves, 34, and still living at home in Stratford Place and working as a clerk in a brassfounder's office. This is the only apparent mention of Jeeves having a fiancée but there seems no reason to doubt Ryder's recollection. So Annie's view was another to take into consideration as the 26-year-old pondered the question faced by hundreds of thousands of men around the country: "Should I go?"

The city of Birmingham was bursting to do its bit for the national cause. During the morning of Saturday 29 August, while Warwickshire were polishing off Surrey at Edgbaston, the Deputy Mayor of Birmingham, Alderman L.H. Bowater, sent a telegram to Lord Kitchener offering to raise and equip a battalion of "young businessmen" from the city. Earlier in the week, Kitchener had told the House of Lords that the war would "demand considerable sacrifices from the people and strain the resources of the Empire". His response to Bowater's offer was immediate. The proposal was "most acceptable".

A local committee went straight to work and across the city of Birmingham, as resoundingly as anywhere in the country, the answer to the above question was "yes". Within a week, two new battalions were filled by more than 4,500 volunteers from not just the business community but a range of skilled trades. They included Warwickshire cricketers Harold and Len Bates (one of 160 sets of brothers in the Second City to join up) and their close friend Percy Jeeves.

30.

Farewell to Edgbaston – Birmingham Pals – Training at Sutton Park – Boldmere Parish Rooms become a lecture theatre

O N SATURDAY 29 August 1914, Percy Jeeves left the field at Edgbaston to a huge ovation from Warwickshire's supporters. He had played for the county for only two full seasons but, during that time, his exuberant, often excellent cricket gave immense pleasure to the spectators. They had taken this talented and courteous young Yorkshireman right to their hearts.

They never saw him play cricket again.

On Saturday 10 October 1914, Jeeves was among thousands of volunteers assembled in the quadrangle of Birmingham General Hospital ready to depart for army training.

The Call to Arms generated a massive response. Across Britain, 100,000 men rushed to enlist in the first two weeks but nowhere were the recruiting offices busier than in Birmingham. Instead of supplying one new battalion, so passionate was the patriotic fervour from the city's white-collar workforce that a second was formed – and then a third.

The region's cricketers donated more than their share of recruits. The *Post* reported that one club alone lost well over a team's worth of men to service of their country: "At a committee meeting of the Knowle & Dorridge Cricket Club it was announced that the following members have been accepted for service in the army: L. Ratcliffe, M.L. Clutterbuck, Stanley Ibbotson, Eric Cashmore, A.F. Whitfield, Wilfred Hughes, N.D. Impey, C.T. Hutchings, J.F.

Harrison, Harold Bower, J. Balkwill, W.K. Hudson, P.L. Patterson, C.L. Hughes, B.A. Peace."

Soon after the season was over, Warwickshire called a special committee meeting at the Colonnade Hotel to which the players were invited to outline their plans. A letter was read out from Lord Kitchener outlining his support for the idea of a Cricketers' Corps, providing a battalion of at least 1,000 men could be formed. That notion never took flight but many of the Bears' players needed no cajoling to join up.

Jeeves attended the meeting and, along with Tiger Smith, Len and Harold Bates, Verner Luckin, Harry Austin and L. Round, expressed an intention to enlist. Smith subsequently failed a medical but Jeeves and the Bates brothers were soon members of the 2nd Birmingham Battalion. P. Jeeves, S.H. Bates and L.T.A. Bates, as they figured in cricket scorebooks, became Private 611 Jeeves, Private 617 Bates and Private 644 Bates of the 2nd Birmingham Battalion, C Company.

Every effort was made by the recruiting officers to keep friends together – these were to be the 'Birmingham Pals' battalions – so the three cricketers were put into not only the same company but the same platoon. They were three of 55 men under platoon commander Second Lieutenant C.L. Jeffery and Sergeant L.H. Lillis.

Jeeves was already firm friends with the brothers who had made him so welcome after he arrived from Yorkshire four years earlier. He was soon to also become very close to a young man from B Company: Private 313 Bridgman.

Charlie Bridgman was serving an apprenticeship at the Austin motor works when he answered Kitchener's call. He loved his cricket and was a capable wicketkeeper so, when a regimental cricket team was formed, he took the gloves – and found himself keeping to one of the best bowlers in the country.

"Caught Bridgman bowled Jeeves" was to become a frequent entry in the battalion scorebook during training at Sutton Park. And while dovetailing in deadly fashion on the field, the two men became firm friends off it. Charlie's son John was to become a lifelong supporter and highly-respected committee member of Warwickshire County Cricket Club.

He recalls: "My dad and Percy were great, great friends. Dad always said that Percy was a wonderful cricketer but just a normal, modest, working-class lad. He thought the world of him.

"The battalion team was quite a good one with Percy and Len Bates in it. My father kept wicket and they played 11 games and won 11. Len would get the runs and then Percy would bowl them out.

"From the moment they met and played cricket together, Dad and Percy really bonded. They were very close and I am not sure, after what happened to Percy in the war, that my father ever had another friend as close. Dad had a long and happy life and was a very sociable man but always spoke of Percy as different – someone very special."

The cricket season was still a long winter away and far from the men's thoughts when Jeeves and Bridgman stood among thousands of recruits gathered on the hospital quadrangle on 10 October. At 3pm, they began to march across the city, led by commanding officer Captain G.H. Smith on his dapple-grey horse and accompanied by the Birmingham Police Band playing 'It's a Long Way to Tipperary'.

A matter of weeks after their daily lives consisted of orthodox jobs in offices, banks or schools or on cricket fields, the men marched through streets lined by cheering people to Steelhouse Lane, then on to Edgbaston Park, on the threshold of training as a military force. The pace of change from a country at peace and simply following the normal routines of summer to one preparing for war was difficult to comprehend.

Next day, the men assembled again at Thorp Street before marching to the Parish Church of St Martin's in the Bull Ring for a service conducted by the Rector of Birmingham, Canon John Willink. That evening was their last at home before training began first thing on Monday.

Their big adventure started with a very short journey. On Monday morning, the new battalions were waved off by thousands of people gathered at New Street Station for their trundle across the city to Sutton Park. The men alighted at Wylde Green and received instructions on the platform.

Sutton Park was to be their base for the next six months but everything had happened so quickly that there were far too few billets in the park itself. Many men were put up in nearby homes as local families did their bit by throwing their doors open to volunteers who were keen to serve their country. Still to be equipped with uniforms, each soldier was issued with an enamel badge to wear as a deterrent to young women who sought to pin white feathers on men they believed to be ducking their national duty.

At 3pm on Monday 12 October, in weak autumn sunshine, Percy Jeeves and 1,069 other recruits assembled for their first parade at Sutton Park. As they stood and saluted on a stretch of open land sloping gently down to Powell's Pool, they had truly arrived in the army. There was no going back now – not that they wanted to. Morale was high and if the sense of "it'll all be over by Christmas" was not quite as all-pervading as myth suggests, there was confidence that they would be back in Brum sooner rather than later.

The Birmingham Pals were originally to have trained at Castle Bromwich Playing Fields but risk of flooding in the Tame Valley caused a switch to Sutton Park. Hurriedly, the infrastructure of a training camp was cobbled together. The 2nd Battalion pitched camp close to the Boldmere and Wylde Green end of the park. The boathouse alongside Powell's Pool became battalion HQ while adjacent refreshment rooms were used as orderly rooms and stores. The Boldmere Parish Rooms became a lecture theatre, the Brotherhood Hall a recreation room.

Guidelines issued by the War Office suggested, with staggering expediency as the Government sought to rush men to France, that it should take six months to turn a civilian into a soldier ready for the front. For Percy Jeeves and the rest of the 2nd Battalion, that process began in earnest at 7am on Tuesday 13 October when they began training under Lieutenant Colonel L.J. Andrews, a veteran of the 79th Carnatic Infantry (Indian Army).

The arrival of uniforms, at last, made the men feel more like a proper military unit and it was in those which the soldiers, two months' training under their belts, dispersed for four days' leave at Christmas. In Kitchener Blue did Percy Jeeves board a train to Goole and disembark at the familiar town station ready to spend Christmas with his family in Manuel Street – for the final time.

31.

Back to Wensleydale – Extricating Young Gussie – Service-rifles are issued – Abide with me

O N THE first day of 1915, the men of the 2nd Birmingham Pals were fully welcomed into the military family when the battalion was renamed the 15th Battalion Royal Warwickshire Regiment. As proud additions to the Royal Warwicks, whose history stretched back to the 17th century, the volunteers trained on through the hostile months of January and February.

The 2,500 acres of Sutton Park have a distinct micro-climate of their own and, during the winter, a particularly harsh one susceptible to bitterly-cold, clinging fogs and persistent rain. Through it all the men drilled and marched and cleaned and cleaned and marched and drilled, adjusting uncomplainingly to the disciplines, discomforts and mundanity of military life.

Practice trenches were dug into Longmoor Valley, an area of rough open heathland on the south-western side of the park. Artillery practice took place in the fields above Powell's Pool. The rookie soldiers drew approval from the new commanding officer of the 116th Brigade, Brigadier-General FW Evatt DSO. He took up residence in Sutton Coldfield and was said to be "favourably impressed" by the men who "were engaged on advanced military work".

On 13 March came an opportunity to show the city how much they had advanced. The battalion paraded at Calthorpe Park, a short distance from the cricket ground on which Jeeves would have been preparing for a new season with Warwickshire. There they were inspected by the portly, handlebar-moustached General Pitcairn Campbell (GOC Southern Command) before marching into the city centre. To the tune of 'Warwickshire Lads and Lasses', they headed into the city, via Five Ways and Broad Street, to the saluting point in Victoria Square. The march-past lasted an hour and concluded with the national anthem.

April brought the men welcome news with regard to accommodation. Having been in temporary billets or nearby lodgings, the 14th and 15th Battalions moved into new 60ft by 20ft huts in the park. The 14th were based opposite the Crystal Palace (Sutton Park's handsome equivalent of the famous original in London – Sutton's version came down in the 1960s) with the 15th still close to Powell's Pool.

The new premises were quickly christened by their occupants who resided at Otazel, Clink-In-View, A-Men, B-Limit, The Dewdrop Inn, Spikanspan, Stan Zie Villa, Be-Jovia, The Nutshell and Some Hut. In these small but basic structures was nurtured the great camaraderie which was to underpin the battalion's stoic and gallant service during the years ahead. Morale was further boosted by a sports day before, in June, the battalion having just passed into the full control of the War Office, the men left the city behind.

If the parade at Calthorpe Park was a poignant location for Jeeves, no less so was his next destination as 12 battalions from Birmingham travelled to North Yorkshire to continue their training in Wensleydale. At 5.45am on Saturday 26 June, the first of two trains carrying the 15th Warwicks departed the Second City. That evening, Jeeves found himself camped in the grounds of Bolton Hall, near Leyburn, just 16 miles from Hawes where that freak sequence of events involving a razor blade and a cricket-loving doctor first propelled him into senior cricket.

Bolton Hall was a handsome 17th-century pile set in beautiful surroundings but, for the next month, life for the 15th Battalion was far from beautiful. Among 12,000 soldiers from a multitude of battalions around the country, the Birmingham Pals were conspicuous, still in Kitchener Blue whereas the rest of the 32nd Division were now in khaki. Day-to-day life was much harsher than at Sutton. Instead of in huts, the men slept under canvas, 16 to a tent. With equipment and kit bags, conditions were horribly cramped. Otazel, The Dewdrop Inn and Spikanspan, back in Sutton Park, were far from five-star but at least boasted beds, sheets and blankets. At Bolton Hall, each man had just a single blanket and groundsheet. Furthermore, it was a rainy month and thunderstorms flooded many tents. The rain also caused trenches, dug in practice, to collapse – little did the men know how prophetic that was.

Rations were meagre and the water supply inadequate. Washing was done in the passing streams and bathing in the River Ure at Wensley. Occasional periods of rest enabled the men to disperse on excursions to the nearby towns of Aysgarth, Redmire and Leyburn but their next destination brought another significant step towards the guise of true soldiers. The battalion headed for the coast and secluded cliff-tops two miles north of Hornsea where, for the first time, they came into contact with guns. Issued with short-magazine Lee-Enfield rifles they spent two weeks firing on the ranges. During the day, the men practised with guns. In the evenings, they attended orchestral concerts in the Floral Hall, Hornsea.

Percy Jeeves's first residence in Wensleydale ended in excitement when he left Hawes to embark upon a career in county cricket. At the conclusion of his second, which lasted a month, there was some excitement, the sense of "national duty" still galvanising the men, but also trepidation. The news from France was bad with the Allies at a standstill on the Western Front.

On Thursday 5 August, the Birmingham battalions, now finally dressed in khaki, moved physically a lot closer to that conflict. They left Hornsea aboard trains which spent the next ten hours trundling south to Wylye Station in Wiltshire. Here, ten miles north-west of Salisbury, was their last base before France – Codford Camp on the southern edge of Salisbury Plain.

First impressions were grim. The 15th Warwicks inherited huts with mud on the floor and filthy cooking utensils strewn around. The previous occupants had evidently left in a hurry.

At Codford, the training became more specific to the conditions awaiting the men in France. The men did arduous tours of duty, day and night. They slept in the open and spent long periods in trenches. They became accustomed to tedious route marches – as testing for anxious minds as for weary legs.

One incentive to get through the slog of training was the prospect of reaching Friday afternoon when special trains left Wylye Station for Birmingham Snow Hill. They returned late on Sunday night so the men could enjoy a full weekend with families and friends before returning to Codford in the early hours of Monday morning. Those who chose not to return to Birmingham visited Salisbury or Bath or stayed local and whooped it up at the Codford Low Down.

It is highly unlikely that anybody at Codford read the 18 September edition of a London newspaper called the *Saturday Evening Post*.

Perhaps one of the officers did, back in the capital. If so, he might have perused a new short story written by P.G. Wodehouse. Entitled *Extricating Young Gussie*, the tale introduced to the world a dutiful manservant by the name of Jeeves. He had just two peripheral lines – "Mrs Gregson to see you, sir" and "Very good sir. Which suit will you wear?" It was a short debut innings at the start of what would become a mighty career for the character whom Wodehouse named after Percy Jeeves.

While the new character was appraised by London literary society, the real Jeeves plugged on through drill after drill in the Wiltshire Downs. As autumn turned to winter, the men of the 15th Warwicks pondered the future. They knew they would soon leave for abroad. But when? And for where? Some rumours suggested they were destined for France. Others said Serbia. Or Egypt.

As October loomed, the battalion was taken over by Lieutenant-Colonel Colin Harding. The son of a gentleman farmer from Somerset, this was, it was assumed, the man who would lead them to France. And sooner rather than later, it appeared, when service-rifles were issued during the second week of October.

During the next month, the 15th Warwicks spent day after day engaged in shooting practice. The men knew the moment of truth was drawing near. In mid-November, they went home on a short leave aware that it was likely to be their last for a long time.

On Friday 19 November, recalled Lt-Col Harding, the soldiers returned to camp armed with gifts galore.

"Leave had been given to the whole battalion," he said, "and tonight, the eve of our departure, they return in twos and threes from their respective homes, laden with delicacies bestowed upon them by affectionate parents and loving friends.

"The battalion is blessed by a devoted and tactful padre. He pays me a visit and as, preparatory to an early morning start, I retire to rest, I hear through my thin-partitioned hut the final verse of 'Abide with me, fast falls the eventide' and with the rhythm of this wonderful hymn in my brain, I slept 'till reveille disturbs…"

32.

A vile introduction to France – Waist-deep thick liquid-mud – Into the trenches – Christmas Day

O N SUNDAY 21 November 1915, the four companies of the 15th Battalion Royal Warwickshire Regiment rose before dawn. They heaved their kit to Wylye Station and squeezed on to two trains which departed at 7.10am and 7.40am, bound for Folkestone.

Percy Jeeves was among 412 members of B and C Companies on the second train as it steamed towards the Kent coast. They reached Folkestone at 4.15pm.

Next morning they boarded the SS *Invicta* and watched England slowly disappear into the distance as the vast vessel, escorted by two destroyers, set out across the English Channel. The *Invicta* had made the journey many times, shuttling men to war, and this crossing was as quick and calm as any. She docked in Boulogne bang on time at quarter to four in the afternoon.

The Governor of Boulogne was there to offer the latest influx of English soldiers a warm welcome. But the first hours spent on mainland Europe by Jeeves and his comrades were anything but welcoming – and far from warm.

Once ashore, the men, headed by two drummers, marched two miles to camp at Ostrohove up on the bleak, windswept hills overlooking Boulogne. With men packed 12 to a tent, each with only a single blanket for cover, conditions were vile, as company commander Major Charles Bill (who reported to battalion commander Lieutenant Colonel Harding) later recalled in his book, *The 15th Battalion Royal Warwickshire Regiment in the Great War*.

With the benefit of over a decade's hindsight, the officer wrote an honest and detailed account of his experiences with the battalion and of their first night in France, he recalled: "It was about the most uncomfortable night we had experienced since our soldiering began. The place seemed inhospitable. No host would think of putting a guest into a damp bed. The blankets we drew were certainly not damp – they were wringing wet.

"When night fell it started to freeze. There was no hot food so we munched bully beef and biscuits and lay on the ground, two and three together, trying to retain the little warmth that remained in our bodies. It was too cold and damp to sleep and eventually we gave up trying and stamped round our bleak hill-top till morning, feeling that our welcome was not as warm as it might have been."

Jeeves and his comrades had no time to dwell on their vile introduction to France. Reveille was at 6.30am. At 8.55am they left the miserable camp behind and, joined by interpreter Captain Louise Nozal, marched to Ostrohove Central Station. Ahead of them was a tortuous journey inland to Longpre, a camp just north of Amiens.

After the laborious process of loading up, the trains left Ostrohove at 10pm and spent hours inching through the dark countryside. Frequently, they ground to a halt to wait at signals, then chugged another few hundred yards before shuddering to a standstill again. Finally, the engines rolled into Conde Station, near Longpre, at half past three in the morning. Wearily, the men disembarked – and immediately marched nine and a half miles to Bellancourt.

There, at last, they rested and Jeeves had some luck. A, B and D Companies were billeted in barns but C Company were accommodated in the grounds of a château. Only the officers settled into the ornate rooms of the stately home, of course, the Other Ranks occupying outbuildings but they could at least enjoy handsome surroundings from their temporary home.

The day of 24 November was one of rest and inspections so, for the first time since leaving Codford, the men of the 15th Warwicks had some time to digest their situation. Their arrival in France brought them bodily much closer to combat but also impacted psychologically. The alien surroundings emphasised how far they were from the comfort and safety of home. Of what lay ahead, they knew nothing beyond the often chilling accounts picked up in snatched fragments of conversation with soldiers passing on the way back from the front.

Then 25 November brought more inspections but less rest as the companies were reintroduced to that bane of the soldier's life – the route march; a pointless yomp from one point to another, designed to make the men fit but which, in practice, often exhausted them needlessly. Such marches helped fill time while the powers-that-be decided what to do with the men.

On 26 November, orders arrived for the 15th Warwicks to move, along with the 12th Gloucesters, to L'Etoile. The weather was turning now and, after a night cold enough to freeze the contents of the men's water bottles, at 8.15am, C Company said farewell to the château grounds. The battalion set off on the ten-mile march to L'Etoile.

They arrived at noon to find the hospitality sparse. "Battalion dismissed to their billets which were very inferior," noted the battalion diary. At least the men were only there for one night. Next morning they marched eight miles to Vignacourt, a town with a population of 20,000 some 30 miles from the front line. Again the welcome was underwhelming. The soldiers arrived in the town square at 1pm and were kept waiting for three hours while local dignitaries finished their lunch. Eventually the men were billeted in houses and barns.

The weather had taken a serious turn for the worse with the nights regularly freezing. On 29 November, rain fell all day to further dampen the spirits of men wondering what lay in store. An ominous clue came from a lecture on how to deal with a gas attack. After the talk, each man tested his helmet by passing through a gas-filled room. The equipment was rudimentary and Jeeves emerged spluttering and breathless like the rest.

December was christened by sustained heavy rain in which the battalion was soon on the move again. At 8.30am on 1 December, they left Vignacourt on a ten-mile march which properly introduced them to one of the biggest torments of soldiers on the Western Front. Every step of every mile was hampered by thick, cloying mud. The sustained marching, allied to increasingly hostile weather, was taking its toll. Eight men were deemed unfit to march so travelled by ambulance. Thirteen had their packs carried.

There was no respite in store as 2 December brought an eight-mile march through quagmires and 3 December another ten punishing miles. This time, ten men rode in the ambulance while 39 had their packs carried before camp was finally reached at Sailly Laurette, a village on the north bank of the River Somme. It is unlikely that Jeeves was among those needing help at this stage as he was such a fit man but Charlie Bridgman recalled that, as the months wore on, Jeeves did suffer badly from the dreaded trench foot.

He was not alone. Private William Bridgeman (no relation to Charlie), of the 15th Warwicks, kept a diary which was later printed in the *Birmingham Evening Despatch* and he recalled those grim days in early December. The discomfort was so intense, he reported, that it overshadowed even thoughts about mortal danger.

"Gradually, almost unconsciously, we became used to the prevailing conditions. The continuous downpour of the last few weeks is followed by intense cold. 'Trench Feet' and the waist-deep thick liquid-mud constitute our greatest menaces. If one happens to step from the centre of the trench without first plumbing its depth with the long 'bean' stick which we all carry, drowning will probably be the un-heroic fate of anyone less than 7ft tall. These awful sump holes are a source of dread and much profanity, especially after dark. The liquid mud tops even our thigh-length gum boots.

"Many of us suffer intense pain due to 'trench feet'. The feet become sodden within the rubber casing and swelling makes the removal of the boots impossible without cutting. Frostbite is accounting for quite a number of casualties. Fighting is occupying our thoughts less and less. Our one desire is to be as comfortable as possible."

At camp in Sailly Laurette, several days were spent simply filling time while orders were awaited. Arms and kit were inspected ad nauseam. A stream of inspections and drills were arranged to keep the men occupied. Spirits were lifted briefly by the arrival of letters from home. Edwin and Nancy, still living in Manuel Street, updated their sports-loving third son with news of his brothers Thomas and Alick, still in Goole working on the railways (a reserved occupation), and seven-year-old Harold. But after the joy of connection with family came the folding up and tucking away of letters and the heart-rending realisation that the people who wrote them were a long, long way away.

Thoughts inevitably turned towards Christmas, just three weeks distant, but on 7 December Jeeves and his comrades had something less pleasant to think about. They were to get their first taste of the front line. Orders came through that the following week they would move up to Suzanne, a small town eight miles to the east, to occupy reserve trenches where they would prepare to go into the front-line trenches at Maricourt a further three miles north.

B and D Companies went up to Suzanne on Monday, A and C Companies following on Thursday. By the time the latter two companies caught up, the former had sustained their first casualties. On their maiden visit to the trenches, for instruction from the Manchesters and Devons, they lost two Other Ranks killed while Second-Lieutenant EG Crisp died of wounds sustained on an "instructional bombing mission".

At 5.15pm on 18 December, a dark, bitterly cold afternoon, the soldiers of C Company marched up to the reserve trenches for their first front-line training. They spent two days there before returning to Suzanne. All the men of the 15th Warwicks were now perceived as trained and ready for front-line duty. And the following day, for the first time, Percy Jeeves went into the thick of it.

At 3.15pm on 22 December, the 15th Warwicks began to move, company by company, in ten-minute intervals to take over billets vacated by the East Surreys at Maricourt. At 4.30pm the relief was completed and, for the first time, the 15th Warwicks took over a complete sector of trenches, A4, the Manchesters to their right, Queen Victoria's Rifles to their left.

Their first taste of trench life was quiet. The German line was disconcertingly close, the two sides separated by No Man's Land mostly measuring between 50 and 150 yards (at one point in Bois Francais, nearby to the west, it was down to five yards) but the opposing armies were content to leave each other alone. For now there was no action and the 15th Warwicks were relieved by the East Surreys on Christmas Eve without a single casualty.

They returned, unharmed, to occupy reserve trenches four miles behind the lines at Suzanne and there, in a barn, did Percy Jeeves wake on his last Christmas Day.

33.

To Arras – "A cold numbness settles upon the limbs" – Jeeves spends his 28th birthday in 24 trench – "Groans and cries were heard"

THE MEN of the 15th Warwicks spent Christmas morning 1915 picking mud off their uniforms and engaged in general cleaning duties. Each soldier received a Christmas pudding, a card and bottle of Bass beer sent by the Mayor and Mayoress of Birmingham on behalf of the city. There were also gifts of much-appreciated woollens – socks, mittens and balaclavas – supplied with love from the Second City. The three battalions of Birmingham Pals were widely known as the Birmingham 'Pets' because of the large amount of comforts sent out to them from home.

A seasonal greeting was read out from the divisional commander General Sir William Henry Rycroft. His words cheered the men less than the doggedly humorous efforts put into a divisional concert party by the Whizz Bangs. It was difficult to get into the festive spirit, though, because everyone knew they were hours away from returning to the front line.

C Company were back in the trenches at 4.30pm on Boxing Day and there they shivered and waited. They laid low under the sporadic crackling of shellfire, any burst of which they knew might be about to land on top of them, but their section of the line was mostly quiet for now. The conflict on the Bray front was at a standstill, with neither side able to come up with a strategy to break the deadlock. On New Year's

150

Eve, the 15th Warwicks' battalion diary reported a "fairly vigorous bombardment" either side of noon with one man slightly wounded. On 6 January, one Other Rank was killed. He joined a British casualty list that had now risen to over half a million, of which 205,000 were killed or missing.

Five days later, the 15th Warwicks were relieved at the start of 18 days' respite from the front. The break began with an eight-mile march west to Morlancourt where the weather turned milder, much to the relief of the men who were camped under canvas. Out of the firing line, they were safer but life remained gruelling. Faced with a daily grind of physical discomfort and mind-numbing tedium, many longed for home. The patriotic zeal which powered the rush to enlist began to be corroded by the interminable rounds of inspections and drills, the apparent lack of a plan and the certain knowledge that they were soon 'for it' again.

'For it', they certainly were after the next orders came through. They were bound for one of the Western Front's most bloody slaughterhouses – Arras. It was an ominous, dreaded destination. And, to get there, they spent day after day hauling back-breaking packs mile after mile through mud. And the winter turned cold again. Bitterly cold. And it began to snow.

On 30 January, the battalion marched ten miles; next day a further 12, north to Talmas. After a week of "general training" they moved six miles south to Coisy where they were introduced to a new weapon, a hand-grenade known as the Mills Bomb (invented and manufactured in Birmingham). On 13 February they relocated again with an 11-mile march through heavy snow to Fourdrinoy where, for a week, ruined houses and barns afforded them modest shelter.

On 25 February, the battalion marched nine miles. The following day, another 18 to Doullens and, after hours inching through thick snow, they arrived to find no hot food awaiting them. The company kitchen was stranded miles back because the horses' hooves could not get a grip on the icy ground. Famished, freezing and exhausted, the state of mind of these men is impossible to imagine.

"Snow blows across the countryside horizontally," wrote Private William Bridgeman. "Halting in this is more trying than moving. A cold numbness settles upon the limbs, giving us the feeling that prolonged inactivity will be fatal. We must keep moving.

"We arrive late and very weary at a town of considerable size [Doullens] and are billeted in the maltings of a brewery. Rations are not issued – the limbers are fast in a snowdrift some distance back, we are told. We hold a consultation, decide it is too late to forage and sleep until ten next morning."

The men spent February 27 snow-clearing while, all the time, snow fell heavily. On 29 February, the battalion marched another eight miles then, next day, slogged on north until finally reaching Arras. The once-beautiful city now lay in ruins, parts of which were held by each army. German soldiers occupied the eastern quarter where opposing sides were separated by only a few buildings amid the rubble.

At 1.15am on 3 March, the 15th Warwicks were among British infantry who relieved the 34th French Division in the front line. C Company occupied the festering brew of snow, water, mud, flesh, blood and vermin which was 24 trench. Here, two days later, Percy Jeeves spent his 28th birthday.

For the next two months the 15th Warwicks alternated between front-line action and reserve positions. They achieved nothing beyond sustaining occasional casualties as the Allies' policy of attrition gnawed away at their own forces as much as those of the enemy. Major Bill recalled the state of perpetual anxiety in which men lived. Any moment could be their last.

"By day, having heard the pop of the cartridge one could usually see the grenades or bombs coming," he wrote, "as they had a high trajectory to drop vertically into the trench and one would usually successfully dodge them if the aim appeared likely to be a good one. But at night, except for some of the bigger stuff which was detonated by a time-fuse which could be seen burning during its flight, it was not possible to see the bomb coming. It was trying to the nerves to hear the pop and to know that something was on the way and to wait patiently for the impact to register a hit or miss."

Added to this fear were constant fatigue, illness and a struggle to keep the cold at bay. The latter was hindered by a customary state of hunger. With supplies short, the men spent much of the time on half-rations.

Even when the enemy artillery was quiet, C Company had to be wary. German snipers prowled day and night, while there was danger too from 'friendly fire'. Shrapnel frequently landed among the British soldiers from their own side's guns fired from behind. Hour after hour was spent lying low in trenches where vigilance was required for another reason: the earth, churned over and over by shellfire, regularly threw up rotting corpses.

Out in No Man's Land, meanwhile, dead Frenchmen remained suspended and decomposing in the wire, denied the dignity of concealment, never mind burial. The rapacious aim of snipers haunted No Man's Land day and night so trying to retrieve fallen comrades from the open ground was fraught with risk.

Even quieter periods were punctuated by outbursts of deadly violence. Just before midnight on 26 March, the 15th Warwicks, provoked by a flurry of rifle-grenade and aerial torpedo-fire, launched a raid. A nine-strong bombing party was dispatched and threw 22 bombs into the German trenches "apparently to some effect as groans and cries were heard from the target area", the battalion diary noted. The bombing party returned at 1.55am without casualties.

Four days later, billeted in Hauteville, a few miles west of Arras, the battalion indulged in some hasty uniform-cleaning and button-polishing before lining up to form a guard of honour to salute commander-in-chief Sir Douglas Haig as he passed through the village. Haig travelled past the rows of soldiers without stopping.

That evening, while Jeeves settled down for another evening in his joyless billets, far away in the Colonnade Hotel, Birmingham, he was in the thoughts – and on the agenda – of Warwickshire County Cricket Club's general committee. They had heard that all was not well with their star all-rounder. The minutes of the committee meeting relate: "The secretary was instructed to write to Mr C.K. Langley with regard to the rumoured illness of P. Jeeves at present with the 15th Battalion Royal Warwickshire Regiment."

Their fears were soon allayed by Langley, a former team-mate of Jeeves in the Bears' bowling attack and who had been assigned to the 15th Warwicks in France on 21 January. At a committee meeting at the Grand Hotel on 4 May, "a letter was read from Lieutenant C.K. Langley with reference to Private Jeeves who had been reported ill by one of his comrades. Jeeves was not actually ill, it appeared. Mr Langley promised to do all in his powers to help Jeeves".

Within 96 hours of lining up to see General Haig driven straight past them, the Birmingham Pals were back at the front. Percy Jeeves was now into his longest stretch at the front so far but, for much of April, it was quiet.

Between 13 and 19 April, only six men of the battalion were wounded, two killed and one left shell-shocked. On 20 April, Arras was heavily shelled by the Germans and the British delivered "vigorous" retaliation. Next day, Good Friday, after 17 days in the firing line, the

15th Warwicks were relieved by the 1st Norfolks. Private 611 Jeeves had survived another tour.

The following week was quiet. With the men billeted at Agnez-les-Duisans, daytime hours were filled with route marches, smoke-alert practices, inspections and drills. The evenings brought an almost-forgotten pleasure – sunbathing. In the first warm weather of the year, the soldiers were able to soak up some sunshine on the riverbank. After months freezing in filth and squalor came the joy of feeling soft, warm air on bodies and limbs. With sunshine always comes a lifting of spirits. Even hope.

The respite was short-lived. On 28 April the battalion returned to the front. Awaiting them this time was trench warfare in all its savagery.

34.

"Murderous fire from the enemy" – A perfect summer's day – Nets strung across the water – B Company is "blown to pieces"

THE 15TH Warwicks began their next visit to the front in the reserve trenches. This was hardly a breeze with its arduous duties of hauling ammunition, tools and barbed wire and shifting huge quantities of wood for shoring up trench walls but it was paradise compared to what awaited them when they went forward again.

At 8pm on 17 May, Major Bill's men began to relieve the 2nd Kings Own Scottish Borderers in K1 sector at Arras. It was a lively part of the line with the trenches under regular fire from trench-mortar and rifle-grenade. In K1, the two armies were separated by around 100 yards of No Man's Land, an ugly mass of craters, wire, broken trees, scorched earth and corpses. The area crackled with menace.

On 19 May a heavy German bombardment left the 15th Warwicks with five casualties. The following three days brought hell.

Both sides had been busy tunnelling under No Man's Land to lay mines and at 5am on Thursday 20 May the Germans detonated a mine which blew up a British device which had been due to be fired at 8pm. The explosions created a huge crater into which A Company of the 15th Warwicks swiftly moved. The new hole was just yards from a German listening post and a potentially valuable spot, so they dug in there and were heavily bombarded for the rest of the day at a cost of two Other Ranks killed and seven wounded.

Throughout the night the Germans continued to bomb the men in the new crater. Next morning, the British responded forcefully with an artillery barrage of their own which began at ten and thundered on without interruption until 5pm. The seven-hour bombardment was intended to knock out the enemy gunners and clear the way for a raid on the German trenches by the 15th Warwicks. Sixty-two men of D Company were selected for the attack. Jeeves and his colleagues in C Company could only thank God they were not chosen. It was a debacle.

When the 62 soldiers went over, at 10pm, they found that much of the damage caused by the artillery barrage had already been repaired by the Germans. Instead of having a clear run at a battered enemy, they found themselves running into a curtain of renewed wire, through which gunfire poured at them. The battalion diary reported: "Parties advanced at steady double towards enemy lines. The German wire, which had been cut by the trench-mortar batteries during the afternoon, had been renewed and wire balls put in. This held up the right party and whilst cutting their way through, the enemy opened up a rapid fire from both firestep and parados. The left party were about a dozen yards from the German trenches when rapid fire commenced.

"Several of the leaders were hit and the order to retire was given. Those who were able regained our own trenches under a murderous fire from the enemy. It is obvious that our enemy had received warning of the raid by some means and had made special preparation to meet it."

From their adjacent positions, the men of C Company could only listen to the onslaught and imagine the fate of their fellows. Initial reports indicated three Other Ranks killed, six missing and 18 wounded with one officer missing, but those figures grew over subsequent hours as wounded men managed to crawl back in from No Man's Land. Others, unable to make it back, perished alone there.

Two days later, the 15th Warwicks, depleted in number and morale, were relieved. Back in reserve at Roclincourt, they digested the contents of a message sent out by Lieutenant Colonel Ryves Currie, General Staff, 5th Division, on behalf of divisional commander Major General Sir Reginald Stephens. It thanked the battalion for gallantry shown during the abortive raid but warned against "injudicious talking throughout the division".

The implication was that the attack, rather than misconceived, had been undermined by loose lips. In some places, the opposing sides were close enough for carelessly loud voices to be picked up but German intelligence was also taking advantage of the River Scarpe. For several weeks, their soldiers upriver had been attaching messages to sticks which were floated downstream to be collected in nets strung across the water.

As casualties continued to rise, at the start of June, the 15th Warwicks consisted of 943 men, almost 100 under strength. On 3 June, Lieutenant Colonel Harding returned to England on leave and Captain Lawrence Bengough took temporary charge. The battalion's last day at the front before relief by the 2nd King's Own Scottish Borderers was due to be June 4. It was a perfect summer's day of unbroken sunshine. And it brought another 115 casualties.

As dawn broke, the sun was out and already strong and, as if in celebration of such a perfect day, all guns remained quiet. Until 4pm.

Two years earlier, to the minute, Percy Jeeves was taking tea with the rest of Warwickshire's players on the opening day of their match against Middlesex at Edgbaston. The Bears were enjoying a good day, having galloped to 143 without loss at lunch then building steadily up to tea. Jeeves hit merrily for 43. Now he and the rest of C Company crouched in their trenches as the silence was shattered by German guns launching a bombardment on B Company immediately to their right.

The sky was pure blue, the air beneath a seething maelstrom of silver and steel, dust and flesh, gunfire and screams as B Company's section was pulverised. They were quickly cut off, their HQ and other dugouts smashed and telephone line severed. For three hours the bombardment continued, shells and grenades raining down on to the stricken men, and Jeeves and his mates could do little more than lie low and pray for their brothers-in-arms.

Finally, just before 7pm, the guns fell silent. When the smoke lifted it was clear from the devastation that many men had simply disappeared – buried alive or blown to bits. Working parties began clearing the area but, just before 9pm, they fled for cover as the Germans launched another bombardment. At 9.15pm they blew three mines. Two exploded harmlessly in No Man's Land but the other detonated directly under C Company's front line. As the British artillery began to respond, among the din of explosions came shouts of warning along the line. It was a raid. This would be a job for bayonets as well as bombs and bullets as more than 500 German soldiers came charging over.

What happened next was later recalled by one of Jeeves's comrades in C Company, Private Harold Drinkwater:

"They opened up again all along the front with artillery of all calibres, our guns replying with equal ferocity. It was pitch dark and shells were leaving backwards and forwards. Shrapnel exploding overhead lit up the trench and by reflections I saw other fellows doing what I was doing, kneeling down against anything that affords protection. This had been going on for some ten minutes when I was conscious of a sudden whirl in the air and knew the barrage had been lifted from our line on to the support. At the same moment it was shouted that the Germans were coming over.

"It will always be a matter of joy to remember how the fellows, all thoroughly well-shaken, jumped out from their different places of cover and got to business with their rifles. This was our first experience of a bombardment practically to ourselves and well it was stood, in spite of the fact that there was no cover. Each man stuck to his post and blazed away into the darkness."

As the Germans charged into B Company's terrain, A and C Companies maintained heavy fire from either side to safeguard their own sections. This was trench warfare in its most direct, terrifying form as German soldiers appeared face-to-face with the British in their own trenches. All the firing and bayonet practice on the ranges at Hornsea and Codford was one thing – this was kill-or-be-killed; a situation to strain the comprehension of men who, less than two years earlier, were clerks, shopkeepers, bank staff, cricketers.

They rose to the life-or-death challenge and eventually the attack was repelled. The raiding party, having taken heavy losses, retreated. Just before midnight the gunfire ceased and silence fell upon a day which had cost hundreds of lives in exchanges from which neither side had gained one inch of ground.

Terry Carter summed it all up in his informative book *Birmingham Pals*: "C Company on the left had suffered few casualties and minor damage. A Company on the right had suffered severely and their trenches were partially wrecked. B Company in the centre had been blown to pieces – all its officers casualties and the trenches completely smashed. Capt Bill, OC C Company, made his way into what was the shambles of B Company front line to try and make contact.

"I found one of the subalterns with about two sections of men and he told me that he thought the rest of the company were all right. It afterwards transpired that he did not know the worst as he and his handful of men were practically all that were left of the company. Their line had been completely obliterated and deep forty-foot dugouts, where most of the officers and men were seeking shelter, had been blown in by eleven-inch armour-piercing shells and the occupants had been killed and buried."

In the early hours of the morning of 5 June, the 15th Warwicks, shell-shocked and grieving, were relieved. The relief was tortuous. On the way up the notorious St Pol Road, the King's Own Scottish Borderers were shelled, causing further casualties and long delays. Even when they reached the front, all movements had to be slow and meticulous because the ruined trenches left the soldiers vulnerable to sniper fire. Not until 4.30am was the relief complete. And then the scale of the carnage became clear.

"As we left the trenches in the early hours," wrote Private Drinkwater, "we left it a mess of a shambles. Most of us possessed pocket torches and whilst some stood on sentry, others went along the remnants of the trenches looking for wounded. Many we found were dead. They made a frightful sight for the most part."

The immediate toll that night, sure to rise, was three officers and 46 Other Ranks killed, two officers and 29 Other Ranks wounded, 27 Other Ranks missing and eight Other Ranks shell-shocked. The roll-call at 8.30 on the morning of 6 June was a heartbreaking affair of many silences.

Two days later the men lined up to hear a message from Major General RB Stephens, commander of the Fifth Division.

"The Divisional Commander congratulates the 13th and 15th Infantry Brigade and the Division Artillery on their work on the night of June 4," he said, "especially the 15th Battalion Royal Warwickshire Regiment and 1st Battalion Norfolk Regiment who, in spite of extremely heavy and prolonged bombardment, prevented the enemy from gaining any permanent advantage from the attack.

"Information from prisoners shows that 500 or 600 of the enemy were employed in the attack which can therefore be looked upon as something greater than a trench-raid. In spite of the mines and bombardment the enemy were repulsed by our first line on far the greater portion of the front attacked. Had not that front line been held with the greatest resolution, it is probable that we should have lost the high ground in E1 sub-sector. The casualties were heavy but would have been much heavier if we had been forced to retake the ground by counter-attack."

The tribute cut little ice with men whose thoughts were of friends lost. Inevitably, too, there was a sense of "there but for the grace of God".

35.

1 July 1916 – Jeeves's last game of cricket – "A vast graveyard with the majority of its occupants exposed to the elements" – "The slaughter going on in Caterpillar Valley"

FTER THE mayhem came some respite for the 15th Warwicks. Their next stretch in the front line, from 11 to 17 June, was mercifully quiet, although Captain Bengough was taken ill and hospitalised. The battalion spent the last two weeks of the month out of the firing line, billeted in huts and ruined houses back in Agnez-les-Duisans. There was a lull in the fighting on the Arras front but the frequent buzzing of reconnaissance aircraft overhead suggested something big was brewing. There was much speculation that a major offensive was planned on the Somme front. That offensive arrived on 1 July and was a catastrophic failure.

The Germans had long expected it and planned for it. For seven days, around 1.6 million shells had battered the German lines while British tunnellers made their way under No Man's Land to lay mines. Two minutes before zero hour – 7.30am on 1 July – the mines were blown. In the minds of the architects of this offensive, the infantry would then simply stroll over No Man's Land and seize the positions of the devastated enemy. The reality was hideously different.

The Germans had dug in so deep they were able to withstand the onslaught. They weathered the bombardment and waited patiently for it to end in the knowledge that they were well-prepared to meet the raid that was certain to follow.

At 7.30am on a sunny Saturday, along a 15-mile section of the Western Front, whistles blew and 66,000 British soldiers climbed from the trenches and began to walk towards the enemy. Within seconds they were met by a blizzard of bullets. Within minutes, thousands of families, oblivious to the catastrophe unfolding miles away across the English Channel, lost husbands, fathers, brothers and sons. Within hours, 20,000 soldiers lay dead and another 40,000 were wounded. The attack was a military blunder of unprecedented and monumental human cost.

The colossal loss of life sent a massive knock-on effect rippling through the British Army across France. Many more men had to be poured into the conflict and on 2 July a runner arrived at Agnez-les-Duisans with orders for the 15th Warwicks. Remote from the carnage of 1 July (C Coy spent the day on fatigue work – "casualties nil … weather fair" noted the battalion diary) they were now destined for the Somme. And their movements towards it over the subsequent three weeks perfectly encapsulate the chaotic leadership of these men and the insane demands made of them.

At 3.30am on 3 July, the 15th Warwicks arrived at Sars-lez-Bois. Accommodation was very limited and many men slept out in the rain. On 6 July, they marched to Moncheaux where they remained for six days, under orders to be ready to move at eight hours' notice. During their time at Moncheaux, on Tuesday 11 July, the men took advantage of some sunshine to play sport. It is highly likely that here, trench foot permitting, Percy Jeeves played his last game of cricket.

The simple joy of playing sport was soon a distant memory as the men were sent upon a crazy catalogue of marches. Early in the evening of 13 July, the vast crocodile (the battalion transport alone occupied three miles of road) set off on a 15-mile yomp. Next day, they moved 18 miles and, next, another eight. On 17 July they covered another seven to Dernancourt where they remained to await orders. When, two days later, those orders arrived, they sent Major Bill and his men to a place which, even amidst the hell-hole of the Western Front, evoked particular dread – High Wood.

They moved up to the Bazentin Ridge and occupied some recently-captured German trenches at Montauban. Visible from there was High Wood, its dense, dark green expanse appearing, from a distance, curiously undamaged amid all the surrounding devastation. It was an illusion. Within the tight phalanx of trees, scorched paths snaked through charred undergrowth littered with the debris of battle. For days, the area had been ravaged by fierce fighting.

The 75-acre, diamond-shaped wood was of huge strategic importance. Its lofted position supplied the best vantage point for miles and the Germans were dug in deep there despite strenuous and repeated attacks by the British. As a result of those failed attempts, much of the land sloping up to the trees was littered with corpses and the air thick with their stench. One cornfield, near the wood's southern corner, was a "field in name only, cratered as it was beyond belief and literally spread with human flotsam that dated back to the July 14th engagements", wrote Terry Norman in *The Hell They Called High Wood*. "It was, in essence, a vast graveyard with the majority of its occupants exposed to the elements." In the heat of summer, the soldiers' discomfort was increased by a profusion of flies and rats.

When the 15th Warwicks arrived in Montauban, the Allies had just missed an opportunity to seize High Wood. Five days earlier, a group of British officers walked up the slopes towards the wood without detection by the enemy. The Germans, off-guard, appeared vulnerable but commanding officer General Sir Henry Rawlinson decided the raid would be too difficult for infantry alone so called for cavalry reinforcements. While the cavalry were coming, the German defences in High Wood were fortified so that when the horsemen arrived and were quickly sent in (the first ever deployment of cavalry in trench warfare) they perished en masse.

Horses and men were slain by a lethal double onslaught of shells launched from Flers, a mile and a half to the north-east, and close-up crossfire from rifle and machine-gunners positioned in two trenches newly-dug nearby. The gunners in those trenches – the Switch Line and Wood Lane – enjoyed perfect firing positions as their presence was almost imperceptible among the land's undulations and further masked by the growing corn and poppies.

The British cavalry and infantry advanced oblivious to this threat. Aerial photographs would have been immensely useful to the attacking force but, though photos taken from reconnaissance aircraft did exist, they were supplied to staff only, back behind the lines, and rarely circulated at battalion level. It was a disastrous night and triggered weeks of futile bloodshed in that tiny corner of the conflict.

Six months earlier, this part of the line was considered cushy. Now it was in the thick of it and, despite appalling losses already, Rawlinson was determined to persist with his quest for High Wood. On 18 July, orders were issued for another major assault to be launched.

Percy Jeeves and his comrades spent the evening of 18 July at Dernancourt. An ominous clue as to what lay ahead of them came from the stream of ambulances which passed through the village all night. Next day they marched up to the line, past the rubble of Fricourt. In his book published 16 years later, Major Bill's recollections were as precise as they were harrowing.

"We moved up Caterpillar Valley to support trenches at its eastern end," he wrote, "Montauban lying to the south of us and Bazentin-le-Grand to the north. The road running up the valley was the main line of communication hereabouts and it was a most unhealthy area. It was packed from end to end with guns of every sort, 9.2 inch, eight-inch, six-inch, 4.5 howitzers, 60-pounders and anti-aircraft guns and literally hundreds of 18-pounder guns, which kept up an almost continuous roar day and night.

"Overlooked by the German positions at Ginchy to the east, it was the target of much artillery fire. There was hardly any cover for the detachments, only holes dug in the ground covered with corrugated iron and earth, which afforded little protection against the Caterpillar Valley barrage which swept relentlessly down the valley at intervals during the day and night.

"Sleep that night was impossible. Shelling was continuous, but far worse was the bark of a 60-pounder battery firing directly over our heads from a position about 30 yards behind us. The ear-splitting crack was terrific and we were so close that we felt the blast every time it fired. That went on right through the night.

"The next day the battalion came in for a little shelling, losing Second-Lieutenant W.R. Pratt (A Coy) and nine Other Ranks all wounded. In the morning we sat tight and watched the slaughter going on in Caterpillar Valley just below us. Guns, ammunition wagons, ration wagons, infantry marching up, wounded walking or being carried down – the road held a continual stream of traffic, with the German guns searching for it. At the cross-roads a quarry was being used as a dressing station. I saw one large shell drop right into it and a dozen or so men came running out but from the number of casualties continually being passed in and out that one shell must have done a lot of damage."

On 20 July alone, in that tiny corner of the Western Front, the 20th Royal Fusiliers sustained 397 casualties, the 2nd Royal Welsh Fusiliers suffered 249, the 5th/6th Scots Rifles 407 and the 1st Cameronians 382.

Among the men watching all this slaughter described by Major Bill was Private 611 Jeeves.

The young man who had once watched his fellow Goole Grasshoppers eating, drinking and laughing on the village green at Luddington and played country-house cricket at Hawes and watched Frank Foster and Jack Hobbs test each other's skills at a great theatre of cricket, peered in disbelief at the atrocities unfolding before him in one tiny theatre of a monstrous war.

36.

The attack begins at dusk – Two companies 'disappear' – Strung out in still rows – Percy Jeeves is missing

G ENERAL RAWLINSON was determined to keep pouring men into High Wood and received support for the strategy from General Haig at a meeting on July 19. The British Army's 13th Brigade, including the 15th Warwicks, was ordered to renew the attack on the German line at Wood Lane. And part of the offensive would be another assault on the wood itself.

To the soldiers of whom this mission was asked, its hopelessness was clear. They had to approach the enemy up gently-sloping open fields, advancing without cover towards well-established, well-concealed gunners. But the orders were intransigent. The offensive would be led by the 14th Warwicks and 1st West Kents with the 15th Warwicks among those in reserve.

Final preparations were made with the dumping of packs and greatcoats and, for the first time since arriving in France, the men of the 15th Warwicks adopted battle order, "this incident alone being sufficiently wind-raising as to what lay before us", recalled Major Bill.

The attack began at dusk. A British artillery bombardment was launched at 8.30pm but was only partially successful against deeply-embedded troops afforded further protection by the thick trees. The shelling was reasonably accurate until the light went but then became more miss than hit in the moonless evening. More German machine-gunners survived than died.

At 10pm, the 14th Warwicks and 1st West Kents went over. Most of the men managed only a few paces before they were cut down. With their star-shells lighting up the valley, the Germans had a perfect view of the enemy lumbering their way towards them ludicrously over-laden. As well as their usual fighting kit, every British soldier had an extra bandolier of ammunition slung round him and carried a canvas bucket full of Mills Bombs. They blundered into the teeth of a storm of shrapnel with barely a chance of firing a shot in reply. The action was tantamount to murder, not by the German machine-gunners carrying out a legitimate defensive act of war, but by the British officers on their own courageous infantry.

As line after line of men were cut down, only a few minutes elapsed before two companies of the 15th Warwicks was ordered to support the attack. C Company, including Percy Jeeves, was one of those chosen.

Even the advance towards battle proved troublesome. A mix-up in communication meant that Major Bill's men stumbled across a trench which they did not know existed – and was already full of British soldiers.

"The night was pitch dark save for the incessant flash of guns and bursting shells and the glare from the star-shells in front," recalled Bill. "And the din of battle all round us was deafening.

"I had overlooked the possibility of there being other trench lines between us and our objective and we had got about halfway when we came across a trench held by the 2nd KOSBs, who were lying in close support. This delayed us badly, as it took some time in the darkness for the file of men to negotiate this deep trench, laden as they were, but eventually we all got across and the remainder of the going was much more easy.

"It is fatal to move quickly in file formation in the dark because of the difficulty of the rear troops keeping touch, but we had the luck to get up through some unpleasant shelling without losing many men."

Any relief at that "luck" was soon obliterated by what his men found next – chilling evidence of the disastrous attack.

"A short distance behind the road which was our immediate objective I called a halt and went forward with one man to find out how the position stood," wrote Bill. "The trench from which the attack had been launched was very narrow and shallow and was obstructed in many places by dead and wounded men. I could learn nothing here as to how the attack had gone, but further along towards High Wood I found a Company of the 14th Warwicks under Captain Bryson. Two of their companies had gone over and simply disappeared, apparently decimated, and they themselves made another effort to reach the enemy line while I was there but were held up by heavy fire and forced to return.

"I told Bryson I would fetch my men up, though what to do with them when I got them there I didn't know. It was obvious from what had happened that the trench which had been attacked was untouched by our gun-fire and to order the Company to attack would mean their utter decimation, as had happened to the 14th Warwicks and the West Kents. Yet we were sent up to support the attack!

"We learned afterwards that at the time of the attack the Germans were carrying out a front-line relief, the trenches, therefore, being doubly manned. I should probably under the circumstances have deemed it my duty merely to occupy the front line and thereby doubtless have incurred the extreme displeasure of the higher command, but the problem was solved for me in an unexpected way."

Amid the storm of flying shrapnel, Major Bill was knocked out cold. He was oblivious to the carnage which intensified around him as the 15th Warwicks pressed on over fields deep with men wounded, bleeding, dead and dying. In *Birmingham Pals*, Terry Carter described the scene: "The men made perfect silhouetted targets under the light from German star shells. The two machine-gun posts situated at either end of Wood Lane criss-crossed No Man's Land like a scythe. The Germans entrenched along Wood Lane stood shoulder to shoulder causing further carnage with rifle-fire and grenades."

On that horrific night at High Wood, the 14th Royal Warwickshires and 1st Royal West Kents bore the brunt. Nine officers and 231 Other Ranks of the 14th Warwicks were listed as killed or missing with a further seven officers and 238 Other Ranks wounded – a total of 485 casualties. The 1st Royal West Kents lost 13 officers and 407 Other Ranks. The 2nd King's Own Scottish Borderers, who supported the attack along with the two companies of the 15th Warwicks, lost 114 men.

"A few Royal West Kents managed to fight their way into the lane and to its fiercely-defended trench," wrote Terry Norman. "It is even said that some Borderers joined them – but no-one remained there unless they were dead.

"Not one of the Royal Warwicks could claim that small consolation, since most of them were strung out in still rows on ground made practically impassable by volume of fire."

Next morning the 15th Warwicks reported one officer and 13 Other Ranks killed, five officers and 90 Other Ranks wounded and one officer and 31 Other Ranks missing.

One of the latter was Private 611 Percy Jeeves. He is still missing.

37.

A brilliant cricketer – "The summit of fame was death" – The Thiepval Memorial – Reverence and affection

A T 72 Manuel Street, just as at thousands of homes across the country, the blinds were drawn. Edwin and Nancy received the dreaded telegram and on 4 August 1916, the *Goole Times*, which once chronicled Percy Jeeves's all-conquering feats on cricket fields, carried the headline: "POPULAR GOOLE CRICKETER KILLED".

Beneath was the following report:

> "It is with deep regret that we have to announce the death of Private Percy Jeeves, son of Mr and Mrs Edwin Jeeves of Manuel Street, Goole.
>
> "He was well-known in Goole as a brilliant cricketer; he formerly played in the Goole Town team, and later with Warwickshire county who, on one occasion, gave him a benefit. At one time he was a prominent member of Swinefleet Football Club.
>
> "He was formerly employed as a clerk by Messrs H. Williamson & Co, hardware merchants.
>
> "Edwin Jeeves, one of the oldest guards in the service of the Lancashire and Yorkshire Railway Company, has been on the Haxey route for many years."

The *Yorkshire Post*, meanwhile, noted that all who knew him would mourn the loss of Jeeves the person as well as Jeeves the cricketer.

"From a cricketing point of view," the paper reported, "his loss to Warwickshire is severe; as a pleasant companion and a modest but wholehearted colleague, his associates in the cricket world will still more regret his death."

At Edgbaston, the news was received with the deepest sadness. First and foremost, a lovely young man had perished, but Warwickshire and England had lost a player who would have adorned their teams for years to come. The prospect of Jeeves and Frank Foster, two all-rounders capable of dazzling with bat, ball or in the field, playing alongside each other for country as well as county would never be realised.

Foster's cricket career was also ended during the war, although in very different circumstances. On 12 August 1915, while motorcycling in Worcester, Foster was involved in an accident in which he suffered a broken leg. The ongoing weakness from that injury, allied to declining mental health, set him along a troubled path through the rest of his life, the last eight years of which were spent in Northampton County Asylum before his death in 1958.

Of the demise of his young fellow all-rounder, whose equanimity and peace of mind he would never know, Foster wrote, with typical flamboyance: "O cruel fate, you robbed Warwickshire of a Barnes and Hobbs rolled into one when you decreed that the summit of fame was death."

The 1917 edition of the *Wisden Cricketers' Almanack*, with its vast obituary section, is one of the most evocative books ever printed. Percy Jeeves had proudly bought a copy of the 1913 and 1914 editions and marked his best feats with pencil. In 1917, the book devoted 60 pages to "Deaths in the war, 1916 – A Roll of Honour." The roll lists 461 men. The 225th is:

"JEEVES Percy (Royal Warwickshire Regiment) was killed on July 22, England losing a cricketer of whom very high hopes had been entertained. Jeeves was born at Earlsheaton, in Yorkshire, on the 5th of March, 1888.

"He played his first serious cricket for the Goole CC and became a professional at Hawes. He took part in Yorkshire trial matches in 1910, but presumably failed to attract much attention. Soon afterwards he went to live in Warwickshire, playing for that county, when not fully qualified, against the Australians and South Africans in 1912. No special success rewarded him in those matches, but in 1913 he did brilliant work for Warwickshire, both as bowler and batsman, and firmly established his position.

"He took 106 wickets in first-class matches that season at a cost of 20.88 each, and scored 765 runs with an average of 20.13. In 1914 he held his own as a bowler, taking ninety wickets in first-class matches, but in batting he was less successful than before. He was chosen for Players against Gentlemen at The Oval, and by his fine bowling helped the Players to win the match, sending down in the Gentlemen's second innings 15 overs for 44 runs and four wickets.

"Mr P.F. Warner was greatly impressed and predicted that Jeeves would be an England bowler in the near future. Within a month, war had been declared.

"Jeeves was a right-handed bowler on the quick side of medium pace, and with an easy action, came off the ground with plenty of spin. He was very popular among his brother players."

The name Percy Jeeves seemed certain to appear on England scorecards. Instead it was engraved upon monuments. It is among 452 names of casualties of the First World War listed upon Goole's Cenotaph which stands in the Memorial Gardens off Boothferry Road. There, one minute's walk from Manuel Street, at the bottom of the right-hand row facing away from the main road, Percy's names sits discreetly among his fellow fallen.

Only Percy's name is there, of course. His remains lie beneath the fields of France. But, in Goole cemetery on the other side of town, his father Edwin rests in an unmarked grave. Percy's mother Nancy died only six years after her third son, in 1922, but Edwin lived to old age. He passed away, aged 79, on 28 October 1941, the place of death listed as 65 Boothferry Road, an address kindly used to disguise the fact that a death had occurred in the workhouse.

Though Edwin died in the workhouse, he was not necessarily destitute. By 1941, workhouses had ceased to be only the last refuge of the penniless which had earned them such stigma. Parts of them simply supplied homes for older people who struggled to look after themselves. Edwin is likely to have fallen into that category.

While he was afforded a plot in the cemetery, however, no monument was placed upon it. Pass beyond the chapels and the Zeppelin Memorial, into the long graveyard as it stretches towards the broad, fast-flowing river, and you will see, immediately to the right of the path, a row of headstones. The line is broken by one space. Under that grass lies Edwin Jeeves.

Percy Jeeves is also one of more than 72,000 names on the Thiepval Monument, a vast memorial to men with no known graves, situated on the site of the Somme battlefield. Carved there, at Pier and Face 9A 9B and 10B, is Jeeves's name, in perpetuity, just a few miles from where his body is lost forever.

How good a cricketer Percy Jeeves would have been will never be known but he littered his brief time with Warwickshire with enough feats of excellence to suggest that his talent, extrapolated over a full career, would have achieved greatness. Almost a decade after Jeeves's death, R.V. Ryder, the man who happened upon the young all-rounder on that walking holiday in the Yorkshire Dales, compared his abilities to those of Foster, the greatest all-round cricketer ever to play for the county.

In *The Cricketer*, in January 1925, Ryder wrote: "Though slight of figure, Jeeves possessed that suppleness and elasticity of frame that enabled him to whip the ball off the pitch at a great pace. Jeeves also bade fare to develop into a dashing batsman of the Foster type. He could hit tremendously hard with little apparent effort. Those who saw it are not likely to forget the magnificent drive that cleared the roof of the pavilion and carried Edgbaston Road, dropping clear in the meadow opposite the main entrance.

"Both as a batsman and a bowler Jeeves was moulded on the lines of his captain. Except that one bowled with his right and the other with his left hand there was little to choose between them concerning that great essential of a bowler – pace from the pitch."

In *Warwickshire County Cricket Club – A History*, written by G.W. Edgell and M.F.K. Fraser (*Birmingham Post* and *Birmingham Evening Despatch* respectively), Jeeves was recalled as "a medium to fast right-hand bowler with an easy action, a lot of life off the pitch and that essential quality of enthusiasm for the game". He was, the authors asserted, "tremendously promising for years to come, though he would probably have been even better if, at this early stage, he had not been called on so much".

That tremendous promise disappeared forever beneath the mud of the Western Front during a conflict which swallowed up much of a generation of cricketers. Among those to lose their lives: Reginald Pridmore (see page 51), Len Taylor (page 66), Arthur Jaques (page 73), Guy Napier (page 80), Colin Blythe (page 81), William Booth (page 85), John Nason (page 88), Bill Tyldesley (page 120) and George Whitehead (page 134). Of the Bates brothers with whom Jeeves played, worked and enlisted, Len survived the war and went on to play 440 matches and score 19,326 runs for Warwickshire but

Harold was killed in action, aged 26, on 28 August 1916, a month after Percy met his death.

Many tributes have been paid to Percy Jeeves's abilities as a cricketer. Of his military service, no specific comment is recorded but all evidence gleaned of his character leaves no doubt that Jeeves was the epitome of the soldier described by Lieutenant-Colonel Colin Harding, in his foreword to Major Bill's book.

"In Africa I have commanded men and more than one unit in France," Harding wrote, "but never have I met or commanded a body of men who were more gentle in manner or more resolute in execution than the Birmingham lads who crossed with me to France in 1915.

"It is with reverence and affection that I shall ever think of those departed comrades, who to the last upheld the loyal traditions of the City of Birmingham and finally without stint gave their young and gallant lives for their Empire and their King."

Harding's words stand as a resounding and richly-deserved tribute to all the men of the 15th Battalion Royal Warwickshire Regiment and, as much as any of its many brave members, to Percy Jeeves. Loyal and gallant, remembered with reverence and affection.

Appendix

The first-class career statistics of Percy Jeeves.

All matches for Warwickshire except one, for Players v Gentlemen, July 1914.

Batting

M	I	NO	Runs	HS	Ave	100	50	Ct
50	81	6	1204	86*	16.05	0	4	49

Bowling

O	M	R	W	B	Ave	5wI	10wM
1492	397	3987	199	7-34	20.03	12	1

County Championship
1913
Batting

M	I	NO	Runs	HS	Ave	100	50	Ct
24	40	2	765	86*	20.12	0	3	23

Bowling

O	M	R	W	BB	Ave	5wI	10wM
780.5	206	2214	106	7-34	20.88	7	1

1914
Batting

M	I	NO	Runs	HS	Ave	100	50	Ct
23	36	4	403	61	12.59	0	1	26

Bowling

O	M	R	W	BB	Ave	5wI	10wM
659.5	182	1658	85	7-52	19.50	5	0

The 50 first-class matches of Percy Jeeves.

1912

v Australia (Edgbaston)	1 and 0	14-3-35-2	
v South Africa (Edgbaston)	9 and 15	4-0-12-1	

1913

v Worcestershire (Dudley)	5	11.4-4-29-3	22-15-23-1
v Leicestershire (Edgbaston)	46 and 23	15.5-7-24-3	12.1-3-37-5
v Derbyshire (Derby)	19 and 36	18-4-48-1	7-0-23-0
v Hampshire (Southampton)	7 and 28	22-7-56-4	25-4-81-3
v Surrey (The Oval)	39	24-9-70-4	11-4-29-1
v Northamptonshire (Edgbaston)	27 and 3	26-7-51-1	24-5-50-0
v Hampshire (Edgbaston)	0	23-3-80-5	16-5-39-3
v Sussex (Coventry)	26 and 29	30.2-12-72-4	18-2-60-1
v Middlesex (Lord's)	43 and 1	19-2-67-1	
v Kent (Tonbridge)	30 and 0	12-5-27-4	7-0-20-0
v Yorkshire (Sheffield)	0 and 42	24-0-88-3	16.2-1-76-4
v Lancashire (Edgbaston)	0 and 6	25.5-7-64-4	27.2-13-55-4
v Gloucestershire (Nuneaton)	4	26.2-6-94-6	21-6-58-2
v Kent (Edgbaston)	3 and 1	27.2-4-90-3	
v Leicestershire (Hinckley)	21 and 50	29-5-109-5	
v Derbyshire (Edgbaston)	7	12-4-21-1	
v Lancashire (Manchester)	1 and 53	21.4-4-84-5	13-1-51-0
v Worcestershire (Edgbaston)	35	22-7-80-3	14.1-5-34-7
v Yorkshire (Edgbaston)	86no	31-10-81-1	
v Gloucestershire (Cheltenham)	1 and 0	17-4-43-0	7-1-12-1
v Surrey (Edgbaston)	11 and 0	22-5-60-5	19-8-30-1
v Middlesex (Edgbaston)	17 and 24no	22-6-64-1	
v Sussex (Hove)	2 and 5	20-5-53-3	
v Northamptonshire (Northampton)	34	15.5-4-51-2	8-2-30-1

1914

v Leicestershire (Edgbaston)	0 and 6	13-4-36-1	17-8-31-2
v Gloucestershire (Bristol)	4	16-8-20-1	11-4-19-2
v Surrey (The Oval)	0 and 7	29-10-109-3	
v Worcestershire (Dudley)	6no	12-4-27-0	16-2-30-3
v Middlesex (Edgbaston)	43no	28.2-7-43-2	
v Middlesex (Lord's)	8 and 0no	19-7-56-2	
v Derbyshire (Edgbaston)	13 and 13	19-7-32-4	

v Yorkshire (Dewsbury)	30 and 10	21-6-54-3	19-4-57-1
v Gloucestershire (Coventry)	0	11-2-27-1	14.4-4-47-4
v Lancashire (Edgbaston)	0 and 30	32-10-75-5	13-7-15-0
v Sussex (Nuneaton)	14 and 5	27-7-62-1	8-3-14-0
v Hampshire (Edgbaston)	10	14.5-5-32-2	22.2-9-33-5
Players v Gentlemen (The Oval)	11	13.2-3-24-1	15-3-44-4
v Northamptonshire (Northampton)	27	27-9-61-3	17-2-47-0
v Northamptonshire (Edgbaston)	0no	11-0-45-0	
v Leicestershire (Hinckley)	1 and 3	26-3-77-2	
v Lancashire (Lancaster)	3	16.3-4-51-6	20-7-55-2
v Worcestershire (Edgbaston)	1	25.4-7-52-7	8-4-7-2
v Yorkshire (Edgbaston)	22 and 0	18-3-67-4	8-0-39-0
v Derbyshire (Derby)	36	18-5-35-4	
v Kent (Edgbaston)	0 and 1	10-1-36-3	7-2-24-1
v Hampshire (Southampton)	6 and 4	23-2-81-1	6-0-20-0
v Kent (Gravesend)	61 and 14	7-1-21-0	8-1-33-1
v Surrey (Edgbaston)	7 and 18	19-4-52-5	21-8-36-2